NEW TESTAMENT GUIDES

General Editor
A.T. Lincoln

1 PETER

Other New Testament Guides available from T&T Clark:

1 Peter

David G. Horrell

t&t clark

Published by T&T Clark
A Continuum imprint
The Tower Building, 11 York Road, London SE1 7NX
80 Maiden Lane, Suite 704, New York, NY 10038

www.continuumbooks.com

British Library Cataloguing-in-Publication Data
A catalogue record for this book is available from the British Library

Typeset by Data Standards Limited, Frome, Somerset, UK.

EISBN 9780567031693

CONTENTS

ACKNOWLEDGEMENTS

My interest in 1 Peter goes back some time, and will continue for some time into the future. In 1995, Ivor Jones invited me to write the Epworth Commentary on the epistles of Peter and Jude, subsequently published in 1998. In 2004, Graham Stanton invited me to write the International Critical Commentary on 1 Peter. I hope that this will be completed within the next decade! I am very grateful to both editors for their encouragement to engage closely in the study of this fascinating letter. Writing this Guide has offered me a good opportunity to further clarify and crystallize my thinking about 1 Peter, and I am grateful to the series editor, Andrew Lincoln, and a former editor at T&T Clark, Georgina Brindley, for enabling me to contribute this volume to the Guides series.

I would like to thank a number of individuals and groups who have helped and supported my work on 1 Peter in various ways. Kelly Liebengood and Andrew Lincoln offered very helpful comments on a draft of this book. Two of my research students, Susan Woan and John White, have provided valuable stimulus through their own projects. Jonathan Morgan and Julianne Burnett have worked on an electronic bibliographical database and generally helped to keep my files in order. Stephen Mitchell very kindly allowed me to use material from the maps in his magisterial study of Asia Minor, and has informed my thinking on the context addressed by 1 Peter through discussion of his own ongoing work and his helpful bibliographical suggestions. Sue Rouillard produced the map. The staff and students of the Department of Theology at the University of Exeter, as always, have provided a happy and constructive environment in which to work. The students who took an evening class on

1 Peter and Revelation offered valuable reflections, as did those who attended my lectures on 1 Peter at the *Vacation Term for Biblical Studies* in Oxford in 2006, where much of the material in this book was tried and tested. Some of my research on 1 Peter, including visits to use libraries in Heidelberg and Cambridge, has been supported by a Small Research Grant from the British Academy, for which I here express my sincere thanks.

Most of all, I would like to thank Caroline, Emily and Cate for making my daily life such a joy: I dedicate this book to them.

David G. Horrell

Exeter, July 2007

ABBREVIATIONS

1QpHab	1Q Habbakuk Pesher (among the Dead Sea Scrolls)
1QS	1Q Rule of the Community (among the Dead Sea Scrolls)
EH	*Ecclesiastical History*
ESV	English Standard Version
LNTS	Library of New Testament Studies
LXX	Septuagint (Greek translation of the Hebrew Scriptures)
NovTSup	*Novum Testamentum*, Supplements
NRSV	New Revised Standard Version
NT	New Testament
SBLDS	Society of Biblical Literature Dissertation Series
SBLMS	Society of Biblical Literature Monograph Series
SNTSMS	Society for New Testament Studies Monograph Series
SNTW	Studies of the New Testament and Its World
WUNT	Wissenschaftliche Untersuchungen zum Neuen Testament

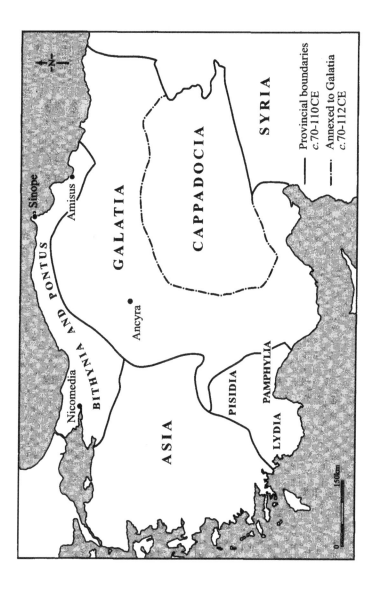

Map: The Roman Provinces of Asia Minor (late first century CE)

INTRODUCTION: RESCUING 1 PETER

1 Peter is among the more neglected letters of the New Testament. Not as neglected as Jude or 3 John, of course, but still rather sidelined in comparison with texts of a roughly similar length, like Galatians or Philippians. The main reasons for this are not too hard to see. Jesus and Paul are the characters who dominate the writings of the New Testament. The four Gospels focus on the life and teaching of Jesus, who is, of course, the central figure around whom Christian theology turns. There are thirteen letters attributed to Paul, not to mention that he also becomes the dominant character in Acts, as the narrative proceeds. Moreover, since the Protestant reformation, and also in historical-critical biblical scholarship - where Protestant voices have been prominent - Paul's theology has taken centre stage. His gospel of justification by faith provides the focal lens through which those in the Protestant tradition have read the Bible and understood Christian theology.

All of that helps to explain why 1 Peter does not receive the same level of attention as letters such as Romans or Galatians. In addition, there has been a tendency in scholarship to regard 1 Peter as a later letter standing in the Pauline tradition - like the Pastoral Epistles (1-2 Timothy, Titus), widely thought not to have been written by Paul but instead by someone claiming Paul's authority and presenting Paul's teaching to a later generation. This view of 1 Peter has added to its relative marginalization, partly through its being subsumed into the more general category of the Pauline tradition, and partly through its being regarded as a later letter of the New Testament and so (rightly or wrongly) less intrinsically interesting for the study of earliest Christianity.

Recent scholarship, however, has gone a considerable way towards rehabilitating 1 Peter from this somewhat marginal status. John Elliott, for example, has consciously sought to rescue 1 Peter from its 'Pauline bondage', that is, to present 1 Peter as a distinctive and important voice among the chorus of New Testament witnesses, and not merely a pseudo-Pauline document reflecting a church that was gradually becoming a more settled institution. Recent studies have sought to appreciate the distinctive character of 1 Peter, and the particular strategy by which the letter seeks to shape the churches to which it is addressed. A number of significant commentaries on the letter have been published in recent decades, all of which have both reflected and developed serious scholarly interest in the letter.

This guide seeks to build upon such work and to continue the process of rehabilitating 1 Peter. First of all, of course, it aims to introduce readers to this letter, to give them a good orientation to the content, context, and concerns of the text, to enable them to read the text with greater insight, and to stimulate their reflection on the issues the letter raises. It also seeks to provide a good indication of the range of ideas and perspectives represented in contemporary scholarship on the letter. But more than that, it aims to constitute an argument for the value and importance of 1 Peter. 1 Peter, I hope to show, is a very interesting and important text in various respects, and a fascinating window onto the development of early Christianity. In particular, it illustrates two fundamental dimensions of the emergence of Christian identity. First, we see in 1 Peter a particularly clear example of the way in which Christian identity was constructed by drawing on the scriptures and identity of Israel. Second, we see in 1 Peter something of the way in which Christian identity was constructed in the face of a hostile outside world, specifically a hostile empire. Both of these aspects of 1 Peter are of considerable historical and theological interest; but they also raise challenging ethical and interpretative questions to which we will need to give some attention. In other words, an argument for the importance of 1 Peter among the documents of earliest Christianity does not mean to imply that the letter raises no issues of theological or ethical difficulty. On the contrary, our response to the letter, I shall suggest, should be critical as well as appreciative. It is worth noting at the outset that this guide to 1 Peter does not proceed by offering a direct analysis of standard facets of the letter's content: its theology, Christology, ethics, and so on. These topics are all included, but they are treated in relation to the two key dimensions of the making of Christian identity – from Jewish sources and in the Roman empire. (The subject index can be used, of course, to locate discussions of particular topics within the chapters that follow.)

The plan for the following chapters is as follows. First, we consider what kind of text 1 Peter is. To what *genre*, or literary type, does it belong? What is the structure and form of the letter? What are its central themes and concerns? Who wrote it, when and where? Second, we examine the range of traditions that are evident in the letter. These include the Jewish scriptures (the Christian Old Testament), and early Christian traditions such as those stemming from Jesus and Paul. Third, we consider what the letter can show us about the situation and identity of the addressees, those to whom the letter was apparently sent. Fourth, we look at one facet of what I have called the making of Christian identity, namely the ways in which Jewish scripture is used in the letter and some of the wider issues that this raises. Fifth, we turn to another crucial dimension of emerging Christian identity, namely, the negotiation of Christian existence in a hostile world. Finally, then, we consider some of the interpretative issues that face us as readers of 1 Peter, and examine some of the contrasting reactions among scholars to this letter.

Further Reading

Literature referred to in the chapters that follow is listed in the various sections giving further reading. All works are cited using the author's name and date of publication.

John Elliott's well-known essay on 'rehabilitating' 1 Peter is mostly taken up with a review of the third edition of the commentary by Francis W. Beare. Nonetheless, it marks a significant turning point in the modern interpretation of 1 Peter, and is well worth reading:

> Elliott, John H., 'The Rehabilitation of an Exegetical Step-Child: 1 Peter in Recent Research', *Journal of Biblical Literature* 95 (1976), 243-54 (reprinted in Charles H. Talbert [ed.], *Perspectives on First Peter* [Macon, GA: Mercer University Press, 1986], 3-16).

Reviews of research on 1 Peter can be found in:

> Cothenet, Edouard, 'La Première de Pierre: bilan de 35 ans de recherches', *Aufstieg und Niedergang der römischen Welt* II. 25.5 (1988), 3685-712.

> Dubis, Mark, 'Research on 1 Peter: A Survey of Scholarly Literature Since 1985', *Currents in Biblical Research* 4 (2006), 199-239.

Further guides to items of bibliography on 1 Peter are offered by:

> Casurella, Anthony, *Bibliography of Literature on First Peter* (Leiden: Brill, 1996).

> Sylva, Dennis, 'The Critical Exploration of 1 Peter', in Charles H. Talbert (ed.), *Perspectives on First Peter* (Macon, GA: Mercer University Press, 1986), 17-36.

For a very recent collection of new perspectives on 1 Peter, see:

> Webb, Robert L. and Bauman-Martin, Betsy (eds), *Reading 1 Peter with New Eyes: Methodological Reassessments of the Letter of First Peter* (LNTS; London and New York: T&T Clark, 2007).

1

WHAT KIND OF TEXT IS 1 PETER?

Since the fourth century, 1 Peter has been known, along with James, Jude, 2 Peter, and 1-3 John, as one of the seven 'catholic' epistles, a designation given officially in Canon 60 of the Council of Laodicea (363 CE [though Canon 60 may be a later supplement to the document]; cf. Eusebius, *EH* 3.23.25). The label was first applied to 1 Peter in the third century by Origen (recorded in Eusebius, *EH* 6.25.5), and was 'used in the sense of encyclical', or circular (Beare 1970: 24, who cites a comment of Oecumenius to this effect). More broadly, the label has been taken to indicate that these letters were regarded as of general appeal and relevance, addressed to the Church as a whole. This is not an altogether appropriate designation of this group of letters, which are quite diverse in character. As we shall see, 1 Peter was addressed to Christians in a specific geographical area, albeit a large one (see Chapter 3); and some other early Christian letters present themselves as of more than local relevance (cf. 1 Cor. 1.2; Col. 4.16) or give no specific indication as to their intended audience (Hebrews). Nonetheless, the description of 1 Peter as some kind of circular letter is valid and useful, and chimes in with modern views of the genre of the epistle (see below).

1 Peter seems to have been accepted without dispute as among the genuine canonical writings of the New Testament (cf. Eusebius, *EH* 3.3.1-3.4.3; 3.25.2; 6.25.8). There is a slight puzzle in the fact that it is not mentioned in the Muratorian Canon, a second-century document from the Roman church, though this is a difficult and somewhat fragmentary text, the date of which is not entirely certain. 2 Peter evidently knows

of an earlier letter from 'Peter' (2 Pet. 3.1; cf. 1.1), though 2
Peter itself is almost certainly by a different author and was
much less clearly or widely accepted by the early church (see
Horrell 1998: 135). Some early Christian writings from the
end of the first century onwards seem to know something of
the content of 1 Peter (e.g. *1 Clement*, usually dated to
around 96 CE), though in many cases it is not absolutely clear
whether there is actual allusion to the text of 1 Peter (see
Elliott 2000: 138–48 for a survey). Polycarp's *Letter to the
Philippians*, written towards the middle of the second
century, contains some clear references to 1 Peter, while
Irenaeus (c. 180 CE) is 'the first writer to cite from 1 Peter
with explicit reference to Peter as author' (Elliott 2000: 146):
'Peter says in his epistle...' (*Against Heresies* 4.9.2).

Our earliest manuscripts of 1 Peter probably date from
around the third century: a codex from the Bodmer Papyrus
collection (the NT texts in this codex, 1–2 Peter and Jude, are
known as P^{72}) and a codex from the Crosby-Schøyen
collection (ms 193). Both of these manuscripts come from
the same early Christian library, but do not reproduce the
same text of 1 Peter. P^{72} is in Greek, and the Crosby-Schøyen
codex is in (Sahidic) Coptic. Generally, the text of 1 Peter is
well attested, including in the important fourth- and fifth-
century uncial codices Sinaiticus, Vaticanus and
Alexandrinus.

The Genre of 1 Peter

'Peter, apostle of Jesus Christ, to the elect refugees of the
Diaspora... Grace and peace to you in abundance' (1 Pet. 1.1-
2). So our text begins, and in so doing adopts the form of the
Greek letter, particularly as adapted to a Christian form by
Paul. The brief, standard opening of a Greek letter gave the
name of the sender(s), the name of the recipient(s), and a
word of greeting. The description of the author as 'apostle of
Jesus Christ' is broadly similar to the opening of some of
Paul's letters (see 1 Cor. 1.1; 2 Cor. 1.1; Gal. 1.1). And the

greeting 'grace and peace to you' is also characteristic of Paul, though he extends the formula by adding 'from God our Father and the Lord Jesus Christ' (see, e.g., Rom. 1.7; 1 Cor. 1.3; 2 Cor. 1.2). Yet there are also differences from the typical Pauline letter opening: the address to the 'Diaspora', that is, to readers scattered across a wide geographical area (see Chapter 3 below), and the verb with which the greeting ends (literally: 'may [grace and peace] abound [to you]'). For these particular characteristics of 1 Peter's opening greeting, closer similarities are found with Jas 1.1, 2 Pet. 1.1 and Jude 2.

Similar comments may be made about the conclusion of the letter (5.13-14), where the greetings, the exhortation to share a 'loving kiss', and the wish for 'peace to all of you who are in Christ' share similarities with Paul's letter-closings (e.g., for the holy kiss, see Rom. 16.16; 1 Cor. 16.20; 2 Cor. 13.12; 1 Thess. 5.26) though they also display their own distinctive features.

All of this would incline one to conclude that 1 Peter is a letter, an early Christian letter following something at least roughly like the form we know from Paul. Indeed it is clear that this is the final form in which the text presents itself to us. However, other proposals have long been made as to the original form of the material in 1 Peter. A popular view, especially in German scholarship from the end of the nineteenth until well into the twentieth century, was that much of 1 Peter originally took the form of an early Christian homily or sermon. W. Bornemann, for example, proposed in 1920 that 1 Peter was a baptismal homily based on Ps. 34 delivered by Silvanus (cf. 1 Pet. 5.12). Later, in 1954, F.L. Cross argued that 1 Peter represented part of the liturgy for the baptismal eucharist celebrated by the early church at Easter. This kind of approach to 1 Peter meant, of course, regarding those parts of the text that are clearly a letter 'frame' – the opening and closing we have examined above – as later additions to this original material. Indeed, during this period of scholarship it was also common to regard 1 Peter as a composite document made up from several originally distinct pieces.

Later manuscript discoveries have in fact lent some weight to certain aspects of these proposals, at least insofar as they concern the identification of the themes of 1 Peter. In both the Bodmer Papyrus and Crosby-Schøyen codices containing 1 Peter, we also find an early Christian text, *On the Passover*, by the second-century bishop Melito of Sardis. The central theme of this text is the way in which Christ is the true sacrificial lamb as foreshadowed in the Exodus account of the Passover (Exod. 12; cf. also Isa. 53). In the Bodmer Papyrus, Psalms 34–35 are also bound in the same codex as 1 Peter, lending some ancient weight to Bornemann's identification of a link between 1 Peter and Psalm 34. But these manuscript discoveries, important though they are, do not prove a specifically liturgical or homiletical origin for 1 Peter. What they do indicate is something of what early readers took to be the central themes of the letter: the suffering, death and resurrection of Christ and their saving effect, and the suffering of God's people in a hostile world.

Indeed, these early theories about 1 Peter as a baptismal homily or an Easter liturgy have now been rather firmly rejected. Already in the 1960s, for example, J.N.D. Kelly could insist that 1 Peter 'is, and always has been, a genuine unity, with a single consistent message, and was written as a real letter to the churches named in the address' (Kelly 1969: 20). Recent commentators have by and large concurred, and regard 1 Peter as a genuine letter (see Elliott 2000: 9-12).

More specifically, 1 Peter may be called a 'diaspora letter', comparable in form and intention with Jewish examples of this genre (see Jer. 29.4-23; Epistle of Jer. [LXX]; Baruch [LXX]; 2 Macc. 1.1-10; *2 Baruch* 78.1-87.1; for Christian examples see Acts 15.23-29; Jas 1.1). A number of these Jewish diaspora letters are associated with the prophet Jeremiah and his scribe Baruch (Jer. 36.4). Importantly for comparison with 1 Peter, they focus frequently on the theme of exile, and are not necessarily sent from Jerusalem to the Diaspora (though this is a common pattern); Baruch (LXX), for example, is said to have been composed in Babylon and sent to Jerusalem (Bar. 1.1, 7). Similarly, 1 Peter is a kind of circular letter, sent to encourage the faithful scattered over a wide geographical area, and sent, so the letter says, from Babylon (5.13) to the Diaspora (1.1). In using these particular terms, the author of 1 Peter draws on Jewish language and tradition (see Chapter 4), but he is applying these terms to Christian believers.

The Structure and Content of 1 Peter

If 1 Peter is, then, a genuine letter, a kind of circular letter, what is the pattern and structure of this text? From the time of some of the early manuscripts, such as the fourth-century Codex Vaticanus, the text of 1 Peter has been divided into sections. Later, of course, our chapter and verse divisions were introduced. Modern commentators also try to determine the structure of the text and to explain its composition, as these are important steps in trying to understand it. Despite some disagreements as to both the structural outline and the compositional principles, which we shall discuss below, there is a reasonable measure of agreement among scholars as to the basic shape of the letter.

The opening of the letter (1.1-2) is clearly distinguished, and follows an established Christian form, as we have seen. The letter continues with a lengthy thanksgiving, a blessing of God for the glorious salvation promised to those who believe (1.3-12). This may be seen as part of the first main section of the letter (1.3–2.10) or as a distinct thanksgiving or blessing section, prior to the body of the letter itself (1.13–5.11). This blessing is full of rich theological language, and it expresses the message and hope of the Christian gospel in a concise yet profound way. For example, what has been given to believers by God's 'great mercy' is 'to be born anew into a living hope through the resurrection of Jesus Christ from the dead' (1.3). The readers are pointed forward, to the fulfilment of their hope (1.4-9), and also told that this promised salvation was foreseen by the prophets of old (1.10-12). Here, too, some of the central themes and concerns of the letter are announced: suffering, joy and hope. It is made clear that the recipients are suffering 'trials' (1.6), but that the certainty of their hope gives them cause for rejoicing, even amidst these pressures. After this declaration of all that God has prepared and is ready soon to reveal (cf. 1.4-5), the letter turns to exhortation, urging the readers to live a holy life worthy of their calling and to turn away from all wickedness (1.13-2.3). The author quotes a prominent refrain from the book of Leviticus - 'Be holy, for I am holy' (cf. Lev. 11.44-45; 19.2; 20.7, 26) - to underscore this instruction, and speaks of their redemption from their previous, futile way of life (1.16-18). This redemption has been accomplished with 'the precious blood of Christ', who is depicted here as a faultless lamb (1.19; cf. Exod. 12.5; Lev. 22.17-25; Isa. 53.7; Heb. 9.14). In a compact and possibly traditional Christological formulation (see Chapter 2), the writer describes Christ as 'destined before the foundation of the world, but...revealed at the end of the ages for your sake' (1.20; NRSV). Again, the recipients of the letter are urged to turn away from all evil and seek nourishment that will enable them to 'grow up to salvation' (2.2).

In 2.4-10 the writer brings 'to a resounding climax the line of thought begun in 1:3' (Elliott 2000: 407). Drawing heavily on the Jewish scriptures (see Chapter 4), he describes Christ as the elect 'stone', chosen by God but rejected by people, and the Church as the elect and holy people of God. Indeed, this section of the letter culminates in a powerful description of the glorious status and honourable identity of this new 'people' (2.9-10).

Most commentators agree in seeing a major break in the structure of the letter at 2.11, where a new section begins. Many see this as introducing a second major section of the letter which runs from 2.11-4.11; others regard it as a section that runs to 3.12, or to 5.11. This new section is marked at 2.11 (cf. again at 4.12) with the word 'beloved' (*agapētoi*). Here the author turns to more practical instruction as to how the Christians are to live in a world where they frequently face hostility and criticism (see Chapter 5). The difficult balance this requires is set out in brief in 2.11-12: on the one hand, Christians must distance themselves from former desires and patterns of conduct, but on the other hand, their conduct must be so 'good' that those among whom they live will recognize it as such.

Drawing on teaching familiar from the Pauline tradition (see Chapter 2), the author urges the readers to conduct themselves properly, submitting to those in authority over them, both in civic society (2.13-17) and in the household (2.18-3.7). All Christians are urged to honour and submit to the emperor and his representatives, though to worship only God (2.13, 17; see Chapter 5). Slaves are urged to be subject to their masters, even the wicked ones, and to accept suffering as Christ did (2.18-25). As a pattern for suffering slaves, and indeed for other Christians too, the author presents a description of Christ's suffering which draws heavily on Isa. 53 (see Chapter 4). Next, wives are urged to submit to their husbands, in order to try to 'win them over' to the faith. (Christian) husbands are also given instruction, to live in an understanding way with their wives, described as 'the weaker sex' (3.7).

These instructions to various groups within the ancient household follow a pattern found elsewhere in the NT (see esp. Col. 3.18-4.1; Eph. 5.21-6.9). Following Luther, this teaching is often referred to as a *Haustafel*, or a household- or domestic code. It has long been recognized that this particular pattern of early Christian teaching has roots in earlier non-Christian traditions of moral instruction. David Balch (1981) in particular has shown how the domestic code in 1 Peter picks up a tradition of teaching about 'managing the household' which goes back to Plato and Aristotle (see further Chapter 5). These instructions, with their ancient presuppositions about the structure of the male-dominated household, as well as their teaching about loyalty to the state, raise difficult questions and issues for contemporary interpreters: How are modern readers to react to this teaching and what is its impact? Does 1 Peter actually keep those who are weak and suffering firmly in their place, and urge them to accept suffering without complaint (see Chapter 6)? This section of practical instruction is rounded off with a series of exhortations concerning the kind of qualities Christians should display in their conduct with one another and with outsiders (3.8-9), followed by a lengthy quotation from Psalm 34 (3.10-12, quoting Ps. 34.12-16).

Again the letter continues with the theme of doing good, even in suffering, following the example of Christ (3.13–4.11); these are the central concerns and themes of the letter. This path of discipleship not only requires the attempt to act in such a way that outsiders will recognize as good (3.13, cf. 2.12) but also distancing oneself from the kind of things 'the Gentiles' do (4.3) and sustaining the life of the Christian community (4.7-11). This section also includes what are undoubtedly the most enigmatic verses in 1 Peter: 3.18-22 and 4.6. These texts have frequently been linked, and seen as referring to the descent of Christ 'into hell', during the time between his death and resurrection, an occasion when the gospel was proclaimed to the dead. However, it is unlikely that 3.18-22 should be interpreted in this way. More plausible is the reading proposed by William Dalton (1989): the imprisoned spirits to whom Christ makes a proclamation are probably the wicked angels, the 'sons of God', described in Genesis 6, and later known as the Watchers (see Chapter 2). What Christ proclaims, Dalton suggests, is not the gospel itself, nor the offer of salvation, but rather his victory over all evil powers. And this proclamation is made on his post-resurrection ascension, not between death and resurrection. This, I think, makes good sense of 3.18-22, which therefore has nothing to do with any encounter between Christ and dead human beings. 4.6, however, remains difficult to interpret. Dalton's proposal is that it refers to those who believed the gospel during their lifetime but have since died. In other words, the concern is similar to that evidenced in 1 Thess. 4.12-5.11: What has become of Christians who have died before the Lord's return? Although this interpretation has been followed in some recent commentaries, it seems to me less convincing than the view that sees here some (admittedly mysterious) announcement of the gospel to people who are already dead (see Horrell 2003).

This section is brought to a close at 4.11 with a brief doxology, an expression of praise to God, which has sometimes been taken to indicate the original ending of a sermon or letter, and thus seen as evidence for the composite character of 1 Peter. However, there is no need to regard the doxology as the conclusion to a letter (see, e.g., Rom. 1.25; 9.5; 11.33-36; Eph. 3.20-21). This doxology marks the end of a section in the letter (2.11-4.11, or 3.13-4.11, depending on the analysis), but it does not prove that an earlier version of the epistle ended here.

In 4.12 the term 'beloved' again marks the beginning of a section of the letter, either the third main section (4.12-5.11) or a further sub-section of the main body of the letter. In the following verses (4.12-19) the situation of suffering is most vividly described, though it has been a theme throughout the letter (see 1.6; 2.19-21; 3.13-17; 4.1). Particularly interesting here is the reference to suffering 'as a Christian' (4.16), since this represents a specific indication about the conflict the readers were experiencing with outsiders (see Chapter 5). Then the author turns to further instruction and assurance, first concerning patterns of relationship and leadership within the community (5.1-5), referring, significantly, to 'elders' as those who bear responsibility for 'shepherding the flock of God' (5.1-2) and then, again, in regard to the need for endurance and perseverance in suffering (5.6-11).

The letter closes, finally, with some personal commendations and greetings (5.12-14). The reference to Silvanus (5.12) is especially significant in discussions of the authorship of the letter (see below). Also significant is the greeting from 'the co-elect one in Babylon' (5.13), since this gives an important indication concerning the place from which the author writes – or, at least, depicts himself as writing – and how he views this place (see further Chapter 5). The word 'co-elect' is feminine in Greek, so the author may be sending greetings from an unnamed woman in 'Babylon', or – more likely, in my view – from the Christian community there (the implied reference may be to the 'church', *ekklēsia*, or to the 'brotherhood', *adelphotēs* [cf. 2.17; 5.9]: both Greek words are feminine).

That completes a brief overview of the content of the letter, but it remains to consider how and why it takes the shape it does and to determine what are its central themes. Among recent attempts to understand the structure and composition of 1 Peter, two approaches may particularly be mentioned.

In a detailed analysis of the literary character of 1 Peter, Troy Martin focuses on its epistolary character, that is, its character as a letter: 'One of the most obvious features of 1 Peter is its epistolary form' (Martin 1992: 41). 'Although the document draws on liturgical, paraenetic, and other materials, all of these have been placed into an epistolary framework' (p. 269). An epistolary analysis shows how 1 Peter 'exhibits the five basic parts of an ancient letter' (p. 269). These are:

1.1-2	'The prescript', which 'identifies the sender and addressees';
1.3-12	'The blessing section', which 'identifies the eschatological context in which the letter is to be read and understood';
1.13-5.12	'The letter-body', which 'contains the message that the author wanted to communicate to his readers';
5.13-14a	'The greeting section';
5.14b	'The farewell' (see Martin 1992: 269-70; cf. pp. 78-79).

As Martin notes (p. 79), while this approach effectively sets out the basic structure of the document, it does not help with the analysis of the extensive 'body-middle', the central section of the letter. To understand the composition of this key section, Martin therefore turns next to an analysis of the form of the letter, identifying its type, or *genre*, as paraenesis; that is, a form concerned with instruction and exhortation about how to live. This kind of writing, Martin claims, 'may be composed around a common theme or motif', and 'this feature proves to be the key for unlocking the Petrine compositional structure' (p. 133).

Martin therefore moves on to examine the metaphor clusters within the letter, seeing these as the key to understanding the structure and composition of the main central section, the letter-body itself. His first major claim is that the 'controlling metaphor of 1 Peter is the Diaspora' (p. 144; cf. pp. 273-74). In other words, '[t]he author of 1 Peter has taken over this conception of Jewish Diaspora life in order to portray the Christian existence of his readers. They have embarked upon an eschatological journey that takes them from their new birth to the eschaton' (pp. 152-53). Within this overarching metaphor, three distinct clusters constitute the structuring principle of the letter-body:

> The first metaphor cluster is built around the image of the elect people of God and contains metaphors pertaining to the house of God (1.14-2.10). The second metaphor cluster is composed of metaphors that group around the notion of strangers and aliens (2.11-3.12). The third metaphor cluster is determined by the concept of the Diaspora as a place of suffering (3.13-5.11). All three of these metaphor clusters are related through the overarching and controlling metaphor of the Diaspora (pp. 160-61).

Martin thus offers a thorough literary analysis of the form and structure of the letter, identifying its central 'metaphor' as the Diaspora. It is, of course, open to question how far we should expect any letter to exhibit a clear 'compositional plan' - and is this a plan intended by the author, or simply a plan that we can discover with (scholarly) hindsight? More specifically, it seems that the important epistolary analysis can reveal only a basic structure of the letter, leaving the central main section (1.13-5.12) in need of further analysis. This Martin provides with his investigation of the use of metaphors, but there perhaps remains room for question as to the extent to which the content of the letter falls under the overall heading of 'Diaspora' and into three sections of related metaphor clusters. As we shall see below, other suggestions as to the central theme(s) of the letter have also been made.

An alternative approach is taken by Barth Campbell, who applies classical rhetorical criticism, combined with a social-scientific approach, to 1 Peter. These two methods have developed rapidly in recent years and become very significant in contemporary New Testament scholarship. Moreover, some, like Campbell, have attempted to combine the two methods into what has been termed a 'socio-rhetorical' approach. The social-scientific side of Campbell's method may be dealt with briefly (see further Chapters 3 and 5 on the social aspects of 1 Peter). Following Bruce Malina, Jerome Neyrey and others, Campbell takes honour and shame to be pivotal values in the ancient world, and sees the recipients of 1 Peter as having suffered a challenge to their honour, being insulted and condemned by those among whom they live. The letter seeks to reassert their honour by depicting them as God's honoured people who will be vindicated by God.

For his analysis of the structure and composition of the letter, Campbell turns to the categories of classical rhetoric, as discussed and presented by the ancient writers on rhetoric, who were concerned with the various ways in which speeches could be made effective. 1 Peter, according to Campbell, is an example of *deliberative* rhetoric, since 'the major sections of the letter reflect exhortation to take future action' (Campbell 1998: 30). The structure of the letter is also to be understood in light of the standard rhetoricians' outline for speeches:

> A proem or exordium that seeks to obtain the auditors' attention and goodwill precedes a narration (*narratio*) of the facts of the case and the proposition (*propositio*) that sometimes features a partition (*partitio*) into separate headings. The proof (*probatio*) contains the speaker's arguments and refutation (*refutatio*) of the opponent's

views. Finally an epilogue or peroration (*peroratio*) sums up the rhetor's arguments and seeks to sway the emotions of the hearers toward the orator's view (p. 9).

This outline, Campbell explains, is based on the standard pattern for 'judicial' rhetoric (concerned with accusation and defence, with the courtroom setting in mind), and was simplified or adapted for deliberative or epideictic rhetoric (the latter concerned with praise or blame for someone's actions).

Campbell's analysis of the letter is then as follows:

1.1-2	'an address that serves as a quasi-exordium' (p. 229);
1.3-12	the exordium, a 'prologue' which is concerned to introduce the matters to be discussed in the speech, to establish a 'positive ethos for the speaker' and 'the attentiveness and goodwill of the audience' (p. 33);
1.13-2.10	First *argumentatio*: these aim to set out and establish what is to be proven. The first establishes 'that the Christian alien residents and visiting strangers of Asia Minor have an honored and dignified position as members of the οἶκος τοῦ θεοῦ [household of God]' (p. 98);
2.11-3.12	Second *argumentatio*, which deals with the way in which the slandered Christians should respond to the challenge to their honour. It constitutes 'the core of the letter' (p. 231);
3.13-4.11	Third *argumentatio*, which 'seeks to persuade [the] hearers that they are honored and that they ought to pursue a course of action commensurate with their privileged position' (p. 233);
4.12-5.14	The *peroratio*, which 'sums up the affirmations and arguments...put forth in 1.1-4.11' (p. 199). 5.12-14 is in fact 'appended to the *peroratio* in order to provide (with 1.1-2) the discourses of 1.3-5.11 with a suitable epistolary frame'; they 'may be classified as a "quasi-peroratio"' (p. 227).

Thus, in the context of a challenge to the honour of the Christians in Asia Minor, and their need to respond to this, the author's composition may be explained by analysing it according to the principles of classical rhetoric: 'Peter operates throughout according to definite principles concerning the invention, arrangement, and style of discourse as these principles found expression in the theoretical treatises on Greco-Roman rhetoric' (p. 235). Not only in the broad structure outlined above, but also in the construction of each *argumentatio*, Campbell sees the principles of classical rhetoric as the basis for the author's formation of his address.

In applying this method to 1 Peter, Campbell is following in the footsteps of many who, following Hans Dieter Betz's pioneering analysis of Galatians in 1975, have undertaken rhetorical analyses of Pauline and other NT epistles. Yet there are questions to be raised about how good the 'fit' is between the categories and forms of classical rhetoric and the content and structure of 1 Peter. First, as with Paul, there are questions to be raised about the educational level of the author, and specifically whether he (or she, but almost certainly 'he') would have been aware of the techniques and forms taught in Greco-Roman education in rhetoric. Second, one may question whether the categories fit as well as Campbell (and others) suggest, and whether they truly illuminate and explain the kind of argument and choice of material the author makes. Is it really right to summarize the exordium (1.3-12) as a section in which the author 'praises his audience' (p. 229), or to suggest that in 3.18-22 the author 'adopts noble and lofty material...that embellishes the argumentation of vv. 13-17' (p. 178), or to suggest that 4.12-5.14 'sums up the affirmations and arguments...put forth in 1.1-4.11' (p. 199)? These and many more examples might suggest that the rhetorical categories are somewhat forced upon the material, and in the end do little to really explain the form and content of the letter.

This comparison of two recent approaches to the structure and composition of the letter also indicates that scholars disagree about what exactly constitutes the central theme or concern of the letter. For Martin, 'Diaspora' is the central 'thematic motif' of 1 Peter (1992: 274), around which the other metaphor clusters coalesce. Paul Achtemeier, however, proposes that 'Israel as a totality' is 'the controlling metaphor' for the theology of 1 Peter (1996: 69; see Chapter 4 below). For Campbell, the dominant subject of 1 Peter is suffering (1998: 33), understood specifically as the loss of social honour (p. 35); thus the aim of the epistle is to restore the readers' honour. For Elliott, whose work we shall discuss further in Chapters 3 and 5, the central motif of the letter is the household of God: the addressees are displaced strangers and resident aliens to whom the author of the epistle offers a new 'home'.

However, these various suggestions as to the central motif of the letter should not be allowed to obscure a considerable measure of agreement as to the main themes and concerns of the letter. For a start, it is clear that the author is concerned to encourage, console and instruct people who are suffering because they are Christians, and that he addresses them using terms drawn from Israel's scriptures and sense of identity (see further Chapters 3 and 4). What exactly are the forms and causes of this suffering is open to more dispute (see Chapter 3). It is also clear that the author presents Christ not only as the one who was destined to come, suffer, die, and rise victorious over his enemies, but also as an *example* in whose steps the suffering recipients of the letter should follow (2.21). Just as Christ bore unjust suffering patiently, and was vindicated by God, so too should the addressees of the letter (2.21-25; 4.1, 13). More specifically, the author urges these Christians to 'do good', to live holy lives, which means being decent and unobtrusive as far as possible, submissive to those who may be 'over' them – emperor, masters, husbands – so as to silence the criticism directed against them, while at the same time remaining firm in their commitment to Christ, even when this brings suffering (see Chapter 5). The hope he offers is based on the conviction that their suffering will only

be for a short time, for the time of final judgement and
salvation is near and certain (1.3-9; 4.7, 17; 5.10). In other
words, the letter is characterized by a strong sense of
eschatological expectation, and this underpins the encouragement the author gives to his readers. Furthermore, he
encourages and affirms the hearers of the letter by assuring
them of their glorious identity as members of God's holy
people (2.5, 9-10): in the world's eyes they may be 'evildoers'
(2.12) but in God's sight they are chosen and special.

The Authorship and Date of 1 Peter

The author of this letter clearly announces his identity in the
opening word of the text: Peter. This Peter is the Simon Peter
(also called Cephas) known from the Gospels as a prominent
member of the group of Jesus' disciples (e.g., Mt. 16.16-18;
Mk 3.16; 5.37; 8.29; 9.2) and from Acts and Paul's letters as a
leading figure in the earliest church (e.g., Acts 1.15; 5.3, 29;
15.7; 1 Cor. 1.12; 9.5; 15.5; Gal. 1.18; 2.7-14). However, since
the early nineteenth century, and the development of
historical-critical approaches to the Bible, this identification
of the author has been questioned. A number of different
views regarding the authorship of the letter have been (and
continue to be) proposed.

First, there are those who defend the traditional view that
the letter was written by the apostle Peter. The letter clearly
makes this claim, and the early church appears to have had no
doubts about accepting 1 Peter as an authentic and apostolic
document (see Elliott 2000: 148-49). Furthermore, it may be
argued that there is nothing in the letter that requires, or even
strongly hints at, its being a pseudonymous composition –
that is, one written by someone falsely claiming the name of
Peter. There may even be some hints in the letter of the
personal experience of Peter, as recorded in the Gospels (e.g.,
the prominence of 'stone' imagery [cf. 1 Pet. 2.4-8; Mt.
16.18], his status as a witness of Christ's sufferings [1 Pet. 5.1;
Mt. 26.37-75]). Those who support the view that Peter wrote

the letter also reject the reasons given below for doubting Petrine authorship, arguing that none is sufficiently weighty to count against the letter's own claim to be by Peter (e.g. Guthrie 1990: 762–81; Marshall 1991: 22–24). If Peter was the author, then the letter was probably written in the early 60s, before or around the time of Nero's persecution (c. 64–65 CE).

However, a number of reasons have been given to doubt this view. One significant factor is the polished Greek written in the letter. It is by no means impossible that Peter knew some Greek, since Greek language and culture had spread across Palestine since the conquests of Alexander the Great. Indeed, Karen Jobes has recently suggested that 'the Greek of 1 Peter arguably exhibits bilingual interference that is consistent with a Semitic author for whom Greek is a second language' (Jobes 2005: 7; see further pp. 325–38). But it seems somewhat unlikely that the fisherman described in Acts as 'uneducated' (Acts 4.13) would produce such a well-crafted letter. Similarly, the quotations from the Jewish scriptures in the letter generally follow the Septuagint, the Greek translation of the Hebrew Bible. Again, it seems more likely that Peter would have known and used the Hebrew versions of these scriptures. Furthermore, there is in fact little indication of Peter's own experience in the letter; the parallels with the Gospel traditions are not extensive, nor do they by any means suggest a particular link with Peter (see Chapter 2 below). (For example, the closest parallels are with sayings from the Sermon on the Mount, preserved in Matthew and in Luke, whereas early church tradition - whether or not it is reliable here - records Peter's reminiscences as being recorded in Mark's Gospel [Eusebius, *EH* 2.15.2; 3.39.15].)

These observations about the letter have led to a second possibility being proposed, namely that Silvanus (named in 5.12) was, in some sense, the author of the letter. This would help to explain the good Greek in the letter, as well as the parallels with Paul's letters, since Silvanus (named Silas in Acts), was a prominent member of the Pauline circle of missionaries (e.g., Acts 16.19; 17.4; 2 Cor. 1.19), and is named as a co-author of 1 Thessalonians (1 Thess. 1.1). This view about the involvement of Silvanus in the writing of 1 Peter is presented in various ways: Silvanus may have worked alongside Peter, more like a kind of secretary (cf. Rom. 16.22); Peter might have communicated his ideas to Silvanus, who then wrote them down in his own style (Davids 1990: 6-7); or perhaps Silvanus had a more active role as a 'joint author' (Selwyn 1952: 9-17). Those who are persuaded by reasons we shall mention below that the letter was written after the time of Peter's death sometimes suggest that Silvanus wrote the letter after Peter's death (Knoch 1990: 22-25).

Indeed, another reason to question whether Peter himself was the author of the letter is the range of indications that it comes from a time when the apostle was already dead. A number of observations may suggest a date after 70 CE, in the last quarter of the first century: the author's use of a wide range of early Christian traditions (see Chapter 2 below) and the indications that Christianity had spread over a large area of Asia Minor (see Chapter 3); the hints of developing structures of leadership (see 5.1-5); the use of the name 'Christian', which appears only three times in the New Testament (1 Pet. 4.16; Acts 11.26; 26.28; see Chapter 5); and the use of the name 'Babylon' to refer (apparently) to Rome (5.13), since the use of this label seems to emerge in Jewish and Christian literature after the fall of Jerusalem in 70 CE (see Hunzinger 1965). Then, of course, the parallels between Rome and Babylon - two empires that attacked the holy city and its temple - become particularly significant. Finally, one may also mention the lack of evidence in 1 Peter for any concern about relations between Jewish and Gentile believers, or about the extent to which Christians should keep the Jewish law, despite the fact that these matters were evidently issues for Peter (see Gal. 2.11-15; cf. Acts 10) and in the Roman churches of the 50s (see Rom. 14.1-15.13; 1 Peter is generally thought to have been written from Rome, see below).

None of these reasons is absolutely decisive, and each may be questioned. However, many scholars have been persuaded that this combination of factors points to a date somewhere around 70-95 CE for 1 Peter, though the suggested range of dates is varied and unavoidably imprecise. If this is correct, then clearly our view of the letter's authorship has to be rethought. One possibility, argued by J. Ramsey Michaels (Michaels 1988: lv-lxvii), is that Peter was not necessarily killed in the persecution under Nero, as is generally thought, but could have been alive to write the letter shortly after 70 CE. This is somewhat unlikely, since early church tradition seems strongly to point to the martyrdom of Peter (along with Paul) under Nero in the mid-60s (e.g. *1 Clement* 5.1-7). That leaves us with the conclusion that someone other than Peter wrote the letter. We have already noted the possibility that Silvanus was the author, before or after the death of Peter. Another prominent theory, developed especially by John Elliott, is that the letter is a product of a 'Petrine circle', a group, including Silvanus and Mark (1 Pet. 5.12-13), based in the church at Rome, who 'knew that they were expressing... the perspectives and teaching of their foremost leader, the Apostle Peter' (Elliott 2000: 130). If one is inclined to doubt the idea that there was such a specifically Petrine group (see Horrell 2002), then we are forced to conclude that we do not know who the author was, nor whether he was or was not especially closely connected with Peter. The letter would then be seen as the product of a Christian author or group, who claimed the name and apostolic authority of Peter for their teaching, but whose identity is likely to remain unknown.

Where was 1 Peter Written?

Although other possibilities have occasionally been suggested, the majority of commentators have concluded that the letter was written in Rome. There are a number of reasons for this conclusion. First, there are the early church traditions that locate both Peter and Mark in Rome, and identify Rome as the place of Peter's martyrdom (see, e.g., *1 Clement* 5.4;

Eusebius, *EH* 2.15.2; 2.25.8; 6.14.6; Bockmuehl 2007).
Second, there is the reference in 5.13 to Babylon, from
where the greetings are sent to those receiving this letter. As
we have seen, Babylon is almost certainly a coded way of
referring to Rome, and a way of identifying Rome as an
imperial power whose impact on the people of God – and on
the city of Jerusalem – can be compared with that of the
earlier Babylonian empire (see Chapter 5). Third, there are
the apparent similarities between 1 Peter and other writings
connected with the church at Rome, especially Paul's letter to
the Romans and the late first-century Roman church's letter
known as *1 Clement*. Most scholars agree that we cannot
show direct *literary* dependence between these texts, but
the similarities do suggest a shared pool of ideas and
knowledge of the same traditions. Finally, it would seem
both appropriate and likely that the Roman church might
send a circular letter to Christians far away. Rome was an
important and increasingly dominant centre of early
Christianity, and we know from *1 Clement* and the
Shepherd of Hermas (another document of early Roman
Christianity) that letters were sent from Rome to churches
elsewhere (Hermas, *Visions* 2.4.3; cf. Ignatius, *To the
Romans* 3.1).

However, a note of caution must at least be sounded. If the
letter is, as many scholars conclude, pseudepigraphical, then
the fact that it *depicts* itself as being written from Rome, just
as it depicts itself as having been written by Peter, does not
necessarily mean that this was actually the case. It is at least
possible that the letter was composed elsewhere, perhaps
somewhere in the regions to which it was addressed, where
the author knew of the particular issues faced by the
churches. Indeed, Claus-Hunno Hunzinger (1965: 77) suggests that the use of the term Babylon to refer to Rome
actually suggests an origin in Syria or Asia Minor; the lack of
'Western' witnesses to the text of 1 Peter and its surprising
absence from the (Roman) Muratorian Canon may add some
weight to this suggestion. Such speculation raises the

question about the addressees of the letter: Who were they and where were they located? Such matters will concern us in Chapter 3, where they will lead us into a consideration of the heart of the letter's concerns in Chapters 4 and 5. First, however, we continue to examine the content of the letter by examining the different traditions on which it draws.

Further Reading

Literature mentioned in the chapter above is listed below, together with brief comments indicating the perspective or argument presented. The major commentaries offer a more detailed review of the history of research, and discussion of the introductory questions of authorship, date, location, etc. Selected commentaries on 1 Peter are also listed below with comments on their scope and perspective.

On the formation of the New Testament canon, including discussion of the Muratorian Canon and other canonical lists, see:

Metzger, Bruce M., *The Canon of the New Testament: Its Origin, Development, and Significance* (Oxford: Clarendon, 1987).

Two examples of the early interpretation of 1 Peter as baptismal homily or liturgical material are:

Bornemann, W., 'Der erste Petrusbrief - eine Taufrede des Silvanus?' *Zeitschrift für die neutestamentliche Wissenschaft* 19 (1920), 143-65.

Cross, Frank Leslie, *1 Peter: A Paschal Liturgy* (London: Mowbray, 1954).

Analysis of 1 Peter as a document of epistolary paraenesis is provided by:

Dryden, J. de Waal, *Theology and Ethics in 1 Peter, Paraenetic Strategies for Christian Character Formation* (WUNT, 2.209; Tübingen: Mohr Siebeck, 2006).

Martin, Troy W., *Metaphor and Composition in 1 Peter*
(SBLDS, 131; Atlanta, GA: Scholars Press, 1992).

Rhetorical analyses of 1 Peter are presented by:

Campbell, Barth L., *Honor, Shame, and the Rhetoric of 1
Peter* (SBLDS, 160; Atlanta, GA: Scholars Press, 1998).

Thurén, Lauri, *The Rhetorical Strategy of 1 Peter: With
Special Regard to Ambiguous Expressions* (Åbo: Åbo
Academy Press, 1990).

Note the criticisms of this rhetorical approach in:

Martin, Troy W., 'Inventing 1 Peter: Interpretive Insights
from Rhetorical Criticism', in Robert L. Webb and Betsy J.
Bauman-Martin (eds), *Reading First Peter with New Eyes:
Methodological Reassessments of the Letter of First Peter*
(LNTS; London and New York: T&T Clark, 2007).

The background to the household code material in 2.11-3.12
is explored by:

Balch, David L., *Let Wives Be Submissive: The Domestic
Code in 1 Peter* (SBLMS, 26; Atlanta, GA: Scholars Press,
1981).

On the origins of 1 Peter, and specifically the suggestion of a
Petrine circle, see:

Elliott, John H., 'Peter, Silvanus and Mark in I Peter and
Acts: Sociological-Exegetical Perspectives on a Petrine
Group in Rome', in W. Haubeck and M. Bachmann (eds),
*Wort in der Zeit: Neutestamentliche Studien. Festgabe für
Karl Heinrich Rengstorff zum 75. Geburtstag* (Leiden:
Brill, 1980), 250-67.

Elliott, John H., *A Home for the Homeless: A Sociological
Exegesis of 1 Peter, Its Situation and Strategy*
(Philadelphia: Fortress; London: SCM, 1981).

Soards, Marion L., '1 Peter, 2 Peter and Jude as Evidence for a Petrine School', *Aufstieg und Niedergang der römischen Welt* II.25.5 (1988), 3827-49.

For criticisms of the idea that 1 Peter is a product of a specifically Petrine circle, see:

Horrell, David G., 'The Product of a Petrine Circle? A Reassessment of the Origin and Character of 1 Peter', *Journal for the Study of the New Testament* 86 (2002), 29-60.

An important and influential essay setting out the evidence that the identification of Rome with Babylon indicates a post-70 date is:

Hunzinger, Claus-Hunno, 'Babylon als Deckname für Rom. und die Datierung des 1. Petrusbriefes', in Henning Graf Reventlow (ed.), *Gottes Wort und Gottesland* (Hertzberg and Göttingen: Vandenhoeck & Ruprecht, 1965), 67-77.

However, arguments against this view are presented by:

Thiede, Carsten Peter, 'Babylon, der andere Ort: Anmerkungen zu 1 Petr 5,13 und Apg 12,17', *Biblica* 67 (1986), 532-38.

On Peter's martyrdom (in Rome) see the recent essay by:

Bockmuehl, Markus, 'Peter's Death in Rome? Back to Front and Upside Down', *Scottish Journal of Theology* 60 (2007), 1-23.

On the interpretation of 3.18-22 and 4.6 see the influential monograph by:

Dalton, William J., *Christ's Proclamation to the Spirits: A Study of 1 Peter 3.18-4.6* (Analecta Biblica, 23; Rome: Pontifical Biblical Institute, 2nd fully revised edn, 1989 [1965]).

A number of the major recent commentaries in English have followed Dalton's view of these verses. For an argument against Dalton's reading of 4.6, see:

> Horrell, David G., 'Who are "the Dead" and When was the Gospel Preached to Them? The Interpretation of 1 Peter 4.6', *New Testament Studies* 49 (2003), 70-89.

There are, of course, many commentaries on the letter. The following is a selection from the range available. Among the older commentaries, influential and valuable works include the following. Kelly is packed with insight for its size and is well worth consulting:

> Beare, Francis W., *The First Epistle of Peter* (Oxford: Blackwell, 3rd edn, 1970 [1947]).

> Kelly, J.N.D., *A Commentary on the Epistles of Peter and Jude* (Black's NT Commentaries; London: A & C Black, 1969).

> Selwyn, Edward Gordon, *The First Epistle of St. Peter* (London: Macmillan, 2nd edn, 1952 [1946]).

Arguments for Peter's authorship of the letter, and a generally evangelical perspective on the letter, can be found in a number of short, accessible recent commentaries. Arguments for authenticity and an early date are also found in Guthrie's *Introduction*:

> Grudem, Wayne A., *1 Peter* (Tyndale NT Commentaries; Leicester: InterVarsity Press, 1988).

> Guthrie, Donald, *New Testament Introduction* (Leicester/ Downers Grove: Apollos/InterVarsity Press, 4th edn, 1990), 760-804.

> Marshall, I. Howard, *1 Peter* (Leicester: InterVarsity Press, 1991).

Among the shorter commentaries, a more critical perspective and view of the letter as later and pseudonymous may be found in:

> Best, Ernest, *1 Peter* (New Century Bible Commentary; London/Grand Rapids: Marshall, Morgan & Scott/ Eerdmans, 1971).

> Boring, M. Eugene, *1 Peter* (Abingdon NT Commentary; Nashville: Abingdon, 1999).

> Horrell, David G., *The Epistles of Peter and Jude* (London: Epworth, 1998).

Medium-length commentaries which offer more detailed discussion and engagement with the Greek text include the following. Goppelt's (originally published in German) is well established as an important commentary. Davids and Jobes both offer a broadly evangelical perspective. Jobes is notable for an analysis of the use of the LXX in 1 Peter and for an argument that the syntax of 1 Peter indicates Semitic influence and an author for whom Greek was a second language:

> Davids, Peter H., *The First Epistle of Peter* (New International Commentary on the NT; Grand Rapids, MI: Eerdmans, 1990).

> Goppelt, Leonhard, *A Commentary on I Peter* (Grand Rapids, MI: Eerdmans, 1993).

> Jobes, Karen H., *1 Peter* (Baker Exegetical Commentary on the NT; Grand Rapids, MI: Baker Academic, 2005).

For those able to read commentaries in French or German, works worth noting include those listed below. Brox's commentary is a standard major work, currently in its fourth edition. The recent work by Feldmeier offers much insight in a short space, building on his earlier work on the letter, though interaction with literature in English (especially some of the major commentaries) is notably limited (there is an

English edition forthcoming, which will make this valuable commentary accessible to a wider audience):

Brox, Norbert, *Der erste Petrusbrief* (Evangelisch-katholischer Kommentar zum NT, 21; Zürich/Neukirchen-Vluyn: Benziger/Neukirchener, 1979).

Feldmeier, Reinhard, *Der erste Brief des Petrus* (Theologischer Handkommentar zum NT 15/1; Leipzig: Evangelische Verlagsanstalt, 2005).

Knoch, Otto, *Der erste und zweite Petrusbrief. Der Judasbrief* (Regensburger NT; Regensburg: Friedrich Pustet, 1990).

Spicq, Ceslas, *Les Épîtres de Saint Pierre* (Sources Bibliques; Paris: Gabalda, 1966).

The most significant recent commentaries on the letter in English are as follows. These are indispensable for the serious student of the letter. All offer detailed engagement with the Greek text and its variants, with ancient parallels, and with the wealth of modern literature. Elliott's is the most recent and comprehensive work, by a scholar much of whose research has focused on 1 Peter and whose commentary therefore encapsulates the fruit of a lifetime's work on the letter. Elliott highlights the social dimensions of the letter's strategy and import, as well as discussing all the other aspects of its historical and theological significance.

Achtemeier, Paul J., *1 Peter* (Hermeneia; Philadelphia: Fortress Press, 1996).

Elliott, John H., *1 Peter: A New Translation with Introduction and Commentary* (Anchor Bible, 37B; New York: Doubleday, 2000).

Michaels, J. Ramsey, *1 Peter* (Word Biblical Commentary, 49; Waco, TX: Word Books, 1988).

2

TRADITIONS IN 1 PETER

1 Peter has long been recognized as, in the words of Ceslas Spicq, 'an epistle of tradition' (Spicq 1966: 15). What this means is that the letter seems to draw on a wide range of Jewish and Christian traditions in constructing its own content and argument. Like the rest of the New Testament writings, 1 Peter does not quote or clearly allude to Greco-Roman literature outside the Jewish-Christian field (for rare examples see 1 Cor. 15.33; Tit. 1.12). The influence of that wider culture and literature is, nonetheless, apparent in both the form and content of the letter – for example in the instruction known as the household code (2.18–3.7). But the most direct connections are with Jewish and Christian texts, which therefore form our focus here. In this chapter, then, we shall look at the uses the author makes of various Jewish-Christian traditions, and consider the implications of these for our assessment of the character of the letter.

Jewish Scriptures and Traditions

Among the writings of the New Testament, 1 Peter is – along with Romans and Hebrews – one of the most saturated with quotations from, and allusions to, the Jewish scriptures, the Christian Old Testament. These may be classified in various ways (see, e.g., Schutter 1989: 35–36; Woan 2004). The most obvious category is *quotations*, which may or may not be introduced with an explicit formula, but are clearly exact or very close reproductions of a scriptural text. Less easily discerned in the letter are *allusions*, where the author appears to reproduce some phrase or part of a text, though these vary in extent and clarity such that some possible allusions remain more uncertain than others. Finally, and with least certainty, one may identify *echoes*, or *biblicisms*, where the author's language might recall a particular biblical story or term, but where this may simply be part of the author's (scripturally-influenced) vocabulary, such that any clear or conscious echo of a specific text is difficult to ascertain.

There are nine quotations from the scriptures in 1 Peter, each introduced with some kind of introductory marker (though this is least clear in the case of 4.18, where 'and' is a somewhat weak and uncertain formula to introduce a quotation). The most clearly marked are 1.16 (Lev. 19.2); 1.24-25 (Isa. 40.6-8); 2.6-8 (Isa. 28.16, followed by Ps. 118.22 and Isa. 8.14); 3.10-12 (Ps. 34.12-16); less clearly marked are 4.8 (Prov. 10.12); 4.18 (Prov. 11.31); 5.5 (Prov. 3.34).

A few examples of some of the clearest allusions are 2.3 (Ps. 34.8); 2.22-25 (Isa. 53.4-12); 3.14-15 (Isa. 8.12-13). In some places characters from the Jewish scriptures are mentioned in ways that obviously allude to the biblical narratives (Sarah: see 3.6/Gen. 18.12; Noah: see 3.20/Gen. 6.14–8.22). Weaker allusions include 2.12 (Isa. 10.3). The potential list of echoes and biblicisms is extensive; indeed, W. Bornemann, in his article claiming that Psalm 34 was the key text on which 1 Peter was based, claimed to find seven quotations and around seventy echoes of this Psalm in 1 Peter (see Woan 2004: 228). Most scholars since, however, have judged Bornemann's case to be vastly overstated.

It may be helpful to set out in detail some examples of these various categories of uses of scripture (see also Chapter 4):

Uses of Scripture in 1 Peter

1 Peter	Scriptural source
Quotations	
For it is written, You shall be holy, for I am holy (1.16).	You shall be holy, for I the Lord your God am holy (Lev. 19.2).

For God opposes the proud, but gives grace to the humble (5.5).	The Lord opposes the proud, but gives grace to the humble (Prov. 3.34 [LXX]).

Allusions

If indeed you have tasted that the Lord is good (2.3).	Taste and see that the Lord is good (Ps. 34.8).
That they may see your good works and glorify God on the day of visitation (2.12).	And what will they do on the day of visitation? (Isa. 10.3 [LXX]).

Echoes

I appeal to you as strangers and aliens (2.11).	I am a stranger and an alien among you (Gen. 23.4).
So that the testing of your faith - much more precious than gold which though perishable is tested by fire (1.7).	Just as silver and gold are tested in a furnace, so are chosen hearts with the Lord (Prov. 17.3 [LXX]).

1 Peter does not contain any direct quotations from non-biblical Jewish texts or traditions, though there are some parallels, and some indications that the author of 1 Peter knew some Jewish traditions of biblical interpretation and expansion. There are, for example, some parallels, both general and specific, between 1 Peter and the writings of the community at Qumran. Both groups had an eschatological outlook - a sense that God's saving intervention would happen soon - and a view of their own community as a holy and elect people in conflict with the wicked world around them. More specific parallels exist in the ways the texts draw upon scriptural texts and imagery to describe the community. A notable example is the echo of Isa. 28.16 in 1QS (the Rule of the Community) and 1 Pet. 2.6:

Therefore thus says the Lord God, See, I am laying in Zion a foundation stone, a tested stone, a precious cornerstone, a sure foundation (Isa. 28.16, NRSV)

It [the Community] shall be the tested wall, the costly cornerstone. Its foundations shall neither be shaken nor be dislodged from their place. (They shall be) a most holy dwelling for Aaron...a house of perfection and truth in Israel (1QS 8.5-9, trans. Charlesworth).

Come to him, a living stone... and like living stones, let yourselves be built into a spiritual house, to be a holy priesthood, to offer spiritual sacrifices acceptable to God through Jesus Christ. For it stands in scripture: 'See, I am laying in Zion a stone, a cornerstone chosen and precious; and whoever believes in him will not be put to shame' (1 Pet. 2.4-6, NRSV).

A different example, showing where 1 Peter is dependent on post-biblical Jewish interpretative traditions, may be found in 1 Pet. 3.19-20. This has proved one of the most mysterious sections of the letter, and has traditionally often been interpreted as referring to Christ's descent into hell, in the days between his death and resurrection (see also 4.6). However, Dalton's (1989) important study has established the relevance of the Enoch traditions (especially those in *1 Enoch*) for an understanding of this text. When the author of 1 Peter refers to Christ's proclamation to 'the spirits in prison...who were disobedient' during the time of Noah (3.19-20) he is probably alluding to the story in Gen. 6.1-5, where the 'sons of God' saw the attractive women born to humans and took those whom they chose as wives. The result of these unions was offspring called Nephilim (giants). The writer of Genesis characterizes this time as one when human wickedness was great, such that God resolved, through the flood, to destroy the earth. This strange story was evidently reflected on in later Jewish literature, and the sons of God mentioned in Genesis 6 (referred to as angels, spiritual beings, or 'the Watchers') were seen as prime examples of evil behaviour, since they transgressed the boundary between themselves and humans (see *1 Enoch* 15.10; also Jude 6).

In *1 Enoch*, a Jewish pseudepigraphical and composite

document, most of which probably dates from 200-100 BCE, there is much reflection on the story of the Watchers, whose actions are seen as bringing corruption and misery to the earth (see *1 Enoch* 6-16). Of specific interest to our interpretation of 1 Pet. 3.19-20 is the statement that these wicked angels will be consigned to 'prison, where they will be locked up forever' (*1 Enoch* 10.13; cf. *2 Enoch* 7, where they are described as tormented prisoners in the second heaven). Dalton therefore argues, I think convincingly, that the 'imprisoned spirits' mentioned in 1 Pet. 3.19-20 are the fallen angels of Genesis 6, to whom the risen Christ, on his ascent through the heavens, announces his victory (3.22). If this is right, then the author of 1 Peter presumes the kind of interpretation of the Genesis stories found in Jewish literature like *1 Enoch*.

Gospel Traditions

There has been some debate about the extent to which 1 Peter echoes material from the Gospel traditions, with some arguing for an extensive use, especially of material linked with Peter and others arguing that only a limited number of allusions are convincing (see the contrasting essays of Robert Gundry and Ernest Best). As with 1 Peter's use of Jewish scripture, it is difficult to determine which possible echoes should be recognized as indicating knowledge of a certain text or tradition. Sometimes they may simply reflect the use of the kind of language that became well established in Jewish and/or Christian tradition – such as calling God Father, or referring to God's people as chosen. All agree, however, that there are some places where 1 Peter echoes sayings from the Gospel tradition, with the clearest examples coming from the Sermon on the Mount: 2.12 (Mt. 5.16), 2.19-20 (Lk. 6.32-34), 3.14 (Mt. 5.10; Lk. 6.22), 4.13-14 (Mt. 5.11-12). Again it may be helpful to set out some of these examples more fully:

1 Peter	Gospel tradition
Conduct yourselves honorably among the Gentiles, so that, though they malign you as evildoers, they may see your good deeds and glorify God... (2.12).	Let your light shine before people, so that they may see your good works and glorify your Father in heaven (Mt. 5.16).
But even if you do suffer for righteousness' sake, you are blessed (3.14).	Blessed are those who are persecuted for righteousness' sake (Mt. 5.10).

These examples make it clear that the author was familiar with this Gospel material, though we do not know in exactly what form. However, in contrast with many of the scriptural quotations, these Gospel traditions are not explicitly quoted or introduced as citations. Rather, they are woven into the text of the letter. Indeed, in other early Christian letters, too, sayings of Jesus are not directly quoted, although some indication may be given that the material comes from 'the Lord' (see e.g. 1 Cor. 7.10-11; 9.14; 11.23-25; 1 Thess. 4.15-17).

Pauline Tradition

For a long time, scholarship on 1 Peter tended to regard the letter as essentially a Pauline text, a pseudonymous second- or third-generation writing somewhat like other later Pauline letters (Colossians, Ephesians, 1-2 Timothy, Titus). If it were not for the name 'Peter' at the head of the letter, it has been suggested, no one would ever have come up with the idea that Peter was the author. Indeed, they would much more likely have thought of it as by Paul. 1 Peter is still presented in some NT Introductions as a letter standing in the Pauline tradition.

However, this perspective on 1 Peter has been strongly challenged in recent years. John Elliott forcefully argues for 'the liberation of 1 Peter from its "Pauline bondage"'. Instead he insists that 1 Peter should be seen as a distinctive product from a Petrine group: '1 Peter is the product of a Petrine tradition transmitted by Petrine tradents of a Petrine circle' (Elliott 1976: 248). Others, such as Jens Herzer (1998), have added their voices to the call to reject the idea of 1 Peter as an essentially Pauline document.

There are nonetheless significant points of contact between 1 Peter and the Pauline tradition. 1 Peter does not simply reproduce phrases or ideas unchanged from the letters of Paul - neither do the Pastoral Epistles - but does in many ways demonstrate close connections with those texts.

We have already mentioned the opening and closing sections of the letter, which exhibit notable similarities with the form found in Paul's letters (see Chapter 1 above). Another small but significant indication of Pauline influence is the use of the phrase 'in Christ' - characteristic of Paul (52 times in the undisputed letters, e.g. Rom. 3.24; 6.11, 23), found three times in 1 Peter (3.16; 5.10; 5.14) but nowhere else in the New Testament. Also found in both 1 Peter and letters of the Pauline tradition are instructions on obedience to the state (1 Pet. 2.13-17; Rom. 13.1-7; Tit. 3.1-2) and on appropriate relationships within the household (1 Pet. 2.18-3.7; Col. 3.18-4.1; Eph. 5.21-6.9; Tit. 2.2-10).

Other specific parallels include the following (and it is not insignificant that these parallels are with Romans, given the dominant view that 1 Peter was written in Rome):

1 Peter	Romans
As obedient children, *do not be conformed* to the desires that you formerly had in your ignorance (1.14).	*Do not be conformed* to this world (12.2). (*Note*: these are the only two occurrences of this verb in the NT)
He himself bore our sins in his body on the tree, so that, being dead to sins, we might live for righteousness (2.24).	Consider yourselves dead to sin and alive to God in Christ Jesus. . .having been set free from sin, you have become slaves of righteousness (6.11, 18).

As each has received a gift, use it to serve one another, as good stewards of God's varied grace: whoever speaks, as one who speaks oracles of God; whoever serves, as one who serves by the strength that God supplies – in order that in everything God may be glorified (4.10-11, ESV). (*Note*: the word 'gift', *charisma*, occurs in the NT only here and in the Pauline letters)

Having gifts that differ according to the grace given to us, let us use them: if prophecy, in proportion to our faith; if service, in our serving; the one who teaches, in his teaching; the one who exhorts, in his exhortation; the one who contributes, in generosity; the one who leads, with zeal; the one who does acts of mercy, with cheerfulness (12.6-8, ESV).

There are also very close verbal parallels between Rom. 12.17, 1 Thess. 5.15 and 1 Pet. 3.9. This exhortation echoes a saying from the Sermon on the Mount (Mt. 5.44; Lk. 6.27-28), so it may also reflect shared dependence on the Gospel traditions. But the precise sharing of words is found only between the three texts in the letters listed above.

What these various examples show is that there are indeed close points of contact between 1 Peter and the Pauline tradition. The parallels do not suggest that there is a *literary* relationship between the texts, such as we see between the three Synoptic Gospels, since the overlaps in wording are generally few and imprecise. But they do suggest that the author of 1 Peter knows and uses in his letter some forms and turns of phrase that reflect some knowledge of Paul's letters. However, this does not mean that we should regard 1 Peter as essentially 'Pauline' in character. As we have already begun to see – in its use of particular texts from the Jewish scriptures, its dependence on the Gospel traditions, and so on – 1 Peter has its own distinctive character, its own particular use of tradition. Further examples of the use of non-Pauline traditions follow below.

Other Christian Traditions

Alongside these indications of 1 Peter's connections with the Pauline tradition, there are also instances in the letter where other early Christian traditions seem to be represented. One clear example is in 5.5-9 where there are striking parallels with Jas 4.6-10.

1 Peter 5.5-9 (NRSV)	**James 4.6-10 (NRSV)**
And all of you must clothe yourselves with humility in your dealings with one another, for "God opposes the proud, but gives grace to the humble". Humble yourselves therefore under the mighty hand of God, so that he may exalt you in due time. Cast all your anxiety on him, because he cares for you. Discipline yourselves, keep alert. Like a roaring lion your adversary the devil prowls around, looking for someone to devour. Resist him, steadfast in your faith, for you know that your brothers and sisters in all the world are undergoing the same kinds of suffering.	But he gives all the more grace; therefore it says, "God opposes the proud, but gives grace to the humble". Submit yourselves therefore to God. Resist the devil, and he will flee from you. Draw near to God, and he will draw near to you. Cleanse your hands, you sinners, and purify your hearts, you double-minded. Lament and mourn and weep. Let your laughter be turned into mourning and your joy into dejection. Humble yourselves before the Lord, and he will exalt you.

Aside from the quotation of the same scriptural text (Prov. 3.34), the similarities here are not so precise as to suggest that one text is literarily dependent on the other – though there are further parallels between the two letters (cf. 1 Pet. 1.1// Jas 1.1; 1 Pet. 1.6-7//Jas 1.2-3; 1 Pet. 1.24//Jas 1.10-11; 1 Pet. 2.1-2//Jas 1.21). What looks more likely is that a pattern of early Christian teaching, drawing on certain Jewish biblical texts, finds expression in both these letters. In other places, too, 1 Peter shares with other early Christian writings a particular interpretation of the Hebrew scriptures, applying these to Christ. One notable example is the Christological reading of various 'stone' texts in 2.6-8 (see below).

Indeed, another kind of Christian tradition that seems to be evident in 1 Peter takes the form of compact Christological confessions. Comparable material is found in Phil. 2.5-11, Col. 1.15-20 and 1 Tim. 3.16. We cannot be sure in these cases that pre-formed traditions, or Christological 'hymns', are being presented, rather than simply the writer's own poetic crystallization of central aspects of the faith. But many scholars, pointing, for example, to the rhythmic and concise expressions in these texts, have suggested that these are indeed instances where some form of established credal confession is reproduced. In 1 Peter there are three passages, 1.18-21, 2.21-25 and 3.18-22, which have long been thought to contain such Christological material (Hans Windisch [1930: 65, 70] referred to them as *Christuslieder*, hymns about Christ). It is notable that when the three texts are considered together, they focus in sequence on the pre-existence and coming of Christ (1.20), his suffering and death (2.21-25), and his resurrection and ascension to glory (3.18-22). In a classic analysis of these texts, Rudolf Bultmann (1947) attempted to identify the earlier forms that underlay these texts. Bultmann argued that a single Christological confession underlay 1.20 and 3.18-19, 22, while a separate hymn was adapted in 2.21-24. It is striking, for example (and here I depart from the detail of Bultmann's proposal), that in 1.20 and 3.18, 22, a series of participles, all passive in form, are used to depict the story of Christ:

> known before the world was made
> revealed at the end of the ages
> put to death in the flesh
> made alive in the spirit
> gone into heaven

It is also striking how the passage about the sufferings of Christ (2.21-25), which draws heavily on phrases from Isa. 53,

is structured with a series of relative clauses, each beginning
with 'who':

> For Christ suffered also for you...
> who committed no sin
> who when abused did not reply with abuse
> who himself bore our sins
> by whose wounds you are healed

It would be implausible to claim that we can confidently
reconstruct the credal formulae that possibly underpin the
author's expression in these texts, though the basic declaration that 'Christ suffered/died for you' is evidently well
established in early Christian tradition (1 Cor. 15.3; 2 Cor.
5.14; 1 Thess. 5.9-10). (The author of 1 Peter tends to use the
verb 'suffered' [Gk: *epathen*] to refer to Christ's passion,
while Paul uses the verb 'died' [Gk: *apethanen*], as in the
examples listed above.) It is unlikely, let it be stressed, that
the key phrases given above as such ever formed an
established early Christian confession of faith. Scholars have
become increasingly sceptical of the kind of rather speculative proposals made by Bultmann, and many have explicitly
rejected the idea that an early Christian hymn underlies 1 Pet.
2.21-25 (see Elliott 2000: 548-50). But it remains likely, even
if we can never reconstruct the details, that the author of 1
Peter drew upon established Christian ways of expressing
beliefs about what God had done in Christ.

Conclusion

1 Peter is indeed 'an epistle of tradition'. Using modern
terminology, we might say that it is richly intertextual, that is
to say, that the fabric of its own text is constructed with the
threads of many other (pre-)texts and traditions woven into it.
The Jewish scriptures provide a pre-text of fundamental
importance for the content and language of 1 Peter. The letter
also reflects a knowledge of a wide range of early Christian
traditions too, all of which shape and influence what the

author writes. As we have seen, there are clear echoes of the Gospel traditions, the Pauline tradition, and other patterns of Christian belief and teaching. One can well see why many authors have seen 1 Peter as bringing together and consolidating diverse early Christian traditions in the church at Rome. That 1 Peter is an epistle of tradition does not, however, mean that we should regard it merely as a collection or synthesis of such materials, lacking much creativity of its own. Far from it. In some cases, the author may be innovative, certainly creative, in the way he draws together and interprets scriptural texts and traditions (see further Chapter 4). More generally, the author's creativity lies in the way in which he draws on all this material to form his own distinctive response to the Christians to whom he writes. Their identity and situation will be the subject for the next stage of our study of 1 Peter.

Further Reading

For analyses of the use of the Jewish scriptures/Old Testament in 1 Peter, see the following studies. Further relevant literature is listed at the end of Chapter 4. Elliott's 1976 essay is listed at the end of the Introduction; the commentaries of Spicq (1966) and Elliott (2000), the essay by Bornemann (1920) and the book by Dalton (1989) are listed at the end of Chapter 1.

Green, Gene L., 'The Use of the Old Testament for Christian Ethics in 1 Peter', *Tyndale Bulletin* 41 (1993), 276-89.

Schutter, William L., *Hermeneutic and Composition in 1 Peter* (WUNT, 2.30; Tübingen: Mohr Siebeck, 1989).

Woan, Sue, 'The Psalms in 1 Peter', in Steve Moyise and Maarten J.J. Menken (eds), *The Psalms in the New Testament* (London and New York: T&T Clark, 2004), 213-29.

On the uses of Gospel tradition in 1 Peter, see the contrasting arguments of:

Best, Ernest, '1 Peter and the Gospel Tradition', *New Testament Studies* 16 (1970), 95-113.

Gundry, Robert H., ' "Verba Christi" in 1 Peter: Their Implication concerning the authorship of 1 Peter and the Authenticity of the Gospel Tradition', *Biblica* 13 (1967), 336-50.

Gundry, Robert H., 'Further Verba on Verba Christi in First Peter', *Biblica* 55 (1974), 211-32.

See also:

Maier, Gerhard, 'Jesustradition im 1. Petrusbrief?' in D. Wenham (ed.), *Gospel Perspectives, Vol 5: The Jesus Tradition Outside the Gospels* (Sheffield: JSOT Press, 1985), 85-128.

Metzner, Rainer, *Die Rezeption des Matthäusevangeliums im 1. Petrusbrief* (WUNT, 2.74; Tübingen: Mohr Siebeck, 1995), who specifically examines the influence of Matthew's Gospel on 1 Peter.

Contrasting perspectives on the Pauline connections in 1 Peter may be found in the essay of Horrell (2002) listed in Chapter 1, which responds to Elliott's view of the letter as the product of a Petrine circle; and in the argument for the independence of 1 Peter from the Pauline tradition presented by:

Herzer, Jens, *Petrus oder Paulus? Studien über das Verhältnis des Ersten Petrusbriefes zur paulinischen Tradition* (WUNT, 103; Tübingen: Mohr Siebeck, 1998).

The analysis of 1.18-21, 2.21-25 and 3.18-22 as traditional confessional or credal material is presented in Bultmann's classic essay, picking up the earlier comments of Windisch:

Bultmann, Rudolf, 'Bekenntnis- und Liedfragmente im

ersten Petrusbrief, in *Exegetica: Aufsätze zur Erforschung des Neuen Testaments* (Tübingen: Mohr Siebeck, 1967 [1947]), 285-97.

Windisch, Hans, *Die katholischen Briefe* (Handbuch zum NT, 15; Tübingen: Mohr Siebeck, 1930).

3

THE SITUATION, IDENTITY AND SUFFERING OF THE ADDRESSEES OF 1 PETER

In the first chapter of this book we considered some of the important initial questions about a text like 1 Peter: What sort of text is it? Who wrote it? And so on. However, we left aside one very important question: To whom is the letter addressed? This question can be answered at a number of levels and has been deferred until now because it warrants a more detailed consideration. It warrants this consideration for two main reasons: first, because an examination of the situation and identity of the addressees of the letter begins to take us to the heart of the letter's themes and concerns; and second, because some aspects of the identity of the letter's recipients have been a focus for debate in recent scholarship.

Their Geographical Location

The letter-opening clearly indicates the areas where its readers are located: 'Pontus, Galatia, Cappadocia, Asia and Bithynia' (1.1). The letter's designation as a 'catholic' epistle is appropriate in the sense that 1 Peter appears as a kind of circular or encyclical letter, sent - or depicted as being sent - from Rome (see Chapter 1) to churches elsewhere. But it is not simply a 'general' letter to all Christians anywhere and everywhere; it has specific geographical areas in view.

The places named, it is widely agreed, refer to the Roman provinces in northern Asia Minor (see Map of Asia Minor on p. ix) and not simply to traditional native regions. Pontus and Bithynia had in fact been merged into a single province from around 65 BCE, under Pompey, but they continued to be mentioned separately in some inscriptions and other sources (Elliott 2000: 84–86; cf. Acts 2.9; 16.7; 18.2). It has often been suggested that the order in which the provinces are listed reflects the likely route taken by the deliverer of the letter – perhaps Silvanus (5.12). If he arrived by ship at the port of Amisus or Sinope (both in Pontus, see Map) he could have made a roughly circular tour round the provinces, leaving from somewhere further west in Bithynia (Elliott 2000: 91, suggests Nicomedia; see Map). Given the wide areas involved, and the likely spread of Christian communities around the region, it has been suggested that the idea of one letter-carrier taking the letter around is implausible (Seland 2005: 9–37). It is possible, then, that the order in which the areas are listed reflects nothing more than 'the author's mental map of Asia Minor' (Jobes 2005: 66). Nonetheless, there seems to me a good deal to be said for the idea of a delivery itinerary influencing the form of the opening greeting – even if the courier's intended route included only selected towns. (Note, for example, how Paul claims that 'from Jerusalem and as far around as Illyricum I have fully proclaimed the good news of Christ' [Rom. 15.19], though he had clearly not covered every area, only certain urban centres.)

Most of the provinces of Asia Minor listed here were somewhat less urbanized and densely populated than the province of Asia itself, which lay at the western side of the region and is also included in the list of areas addressed. Here we find the cities to which John of Patmos wrote his seven letters (Rev. 2–3). It is also notable that the provinces to which 1 Peter was addressed were largely outside the areas in which Paul's mission was conducted; the places Paul visited were further to the south and west of the region (e.g. Ephesus [1 Cor. 16.8], Troas [2 Cor. 2.12]. See the maps of Paul's journeys in many Bibles, though it needs to be noted that most of the information concerning places visited and routes taken derives from Acts, not from Paul's own accounts. Interestingly, Acts 16.7 refers to Paul and Timothy being prevented by the Spirit from going into Bithynia). So we know from the letter where, in a broad sense, its recipients were located. We now need to ask what more we can deduce about them.

Their Ethnic/Religious Identity: Jews or Gentiles?

The opening verse of 1 Peter not only names the provinces in which the readers are located but also addresses them as 'the elect strangers of the Diaspora'. These terms derive from Jewish tradition and show how the writer's thought and expression is thoroughly infused with Jewish scriptural language (see further Chapter 4). The people of Israel are frequently described in the Jewish scriptures as 'chosen', or 'elect', and the idea that God's people live as strangers and aliens is also a common motif (see next section). The term Diaspora, a transliteration of the Greek word meaning 'dispersion', is the word used specifically to refer to the scattering of the Jews throughout the nations of the world, away from their ancestral homeland. Moreover, as we have already seen, 1 Peter is a letter particularly saturated with quotations and allusions to the Jewish scriptures, and as we shall see in the next chapter, the writer of 1 Peter uses thoroughly biblical and Jewish terms to describe the identity of the people to whom he is writing. All of this helps to explain why figures in the early church (e.g., Eusebius, *EH* 3.1.2; 3.4.2; Jerome, *On the Lives of Illustrious Men* 1 [on Simon Peter]), and later interpreters such as Calvin and Wesley, took the letter to be addressed to *Jewish* converts.

However, recent commentators have tended to argue that the letter is addressed to (mostly) Gentile converts, given the ways in which it depicts their former lifestyle. Particularly significant are references to their 'former ignorance' (1.14), to being ransomed from 'futile ways' (1.18), once 'not a people...now God's people' (2.10), and especially to their having spent time enough living like the Gentiles do (4.3-4). The author depicts this as a wicked and debauched lifestyle,

and comments that their neighbours are surprised that they
no longer join in. While it is perhaps not impossible that the
author depicted Jewish converts in these ways (so Jobes
2005: 23-24), it seems highly unlikely, and much more likely
to refer to people who have converted from a Gentile way of
life, which Jews not infrequently criticized as idolatrous and
immoral (e.g. Deut. 29.16-18; Isa. 46.1-10; Wis. 13-15; 1
Macc. 1.41-64; Bel 1.1-22). The letter, then, seems to
envisage, or imply, an audience of Gentile converts
(Bechtler 1998: 61-64).

   Whether the churches that read this letter were actually
composed of Gentile or Jewish converts, or both, is difficult
to know, since we have no direct evidence concerning the
communities that received the letter, apart from the internal
evidence of the text itself. We do know that there were
significant numbers of Jews in Asia Minor (see Trebilco 1991),
so there could certainly have been Jewish converts in the
churches; and some (or many) of the Gentile converts may
have previously been 'Godfearers' – adherents and sympathi-
zers connected with the Jewish communities, but not full
converts to Judaism. Obviously, converts with some prior
knowledge of Judaism and its scriptures would have been
better placed to understand the letter than those without
such knowledge. But aside from such generalizations it is
difficult to be sure. Probably the best guess is that the
churches that received the letter were largely, but by no
means exclusively, Gentile in composition.

Their Socio-political Identity: Aliens and Strangers

The letter gives us few clues as to the social and economic
position of the readers. It is clear that there were slaves,
specifically household slaves (*oiketai*), among the readers
(2.18-20) and the lack of instruction to masters (contrast Col.
4.1; Eph. 6.9) might indicate that those of the slave-owning
class were not included among the congregations. However,
this is not a very convincing argument; instructions to masters

as such are also absent from the Pastoral Epistles (cf. 1 Tim.
6.1-2; Tit. 2.9-10), but here it is clear that some of those
addressed as leaders in the churches are heads of households,
who are expected to keep wives, children and slaves in order
(1 Tim. 3.12). In 1 Peter there is no mention of 'bishops'
(*episkopoi*) or 'deacons' (*diakonoi*), but there is reference to
'elders' (*presbyteroi*, 5.1, 5; cf. 1 Tim. 5.1-2, 17-19; Tit. 1.5),
whose task includes 'overseeing' (*episkopountes*) the flock
(5.2). Alastair Campbell (1994) has argued that these elders
were the senior members of the churches, not only in age but
also in social position – heads of household who hosted the
meetings of the earliest house churches and, in time, became
the overseers of the churches in their towns. 1 Peter also
refers to Christian wives, some of whom apparently had non-
Christian husbands (3.1-6); but there were also Christian
husbands among the members of the churches (3.7).
Although we cannot be sure, it seems likely that there were
whole households and families within the congregations,
husbands and masters as well as slaves and wives. The letter
gives us very few clues from which to deduce anything much
about their likely social level. It is notable, however, that
Pliny, the governor of Pontus-Bithynia early in the second
century, when writing to the emperor Trajan about the
Christians (see Chapter 5 below), says that the Christians
came from 'every age, every class, and both sexes' (Pliny,
Letters 10.96). This was probably written up to two or three
decades after 1 Peter, but clearly gives the impression that
Christianity had spread widely through all strata of the
population. Although the numbers of Christians may have
been somewhat smaller in 1 Peter's time, it is reasonable to
suppose that Pliny's picture of the Christian movement's
broad social appeal is more or less accurate for the time of the
letter too.

What is more difficult to say is whether the Christians
addressed lived mostly in towns or in the country. It is often
noted that the provinces to which 1 Peter was addressed
were less urbanized than the western province of Asia, with

its cluster of coastal towns. Indeed, Elliott (1981: 59-65) has argued that 'the letter is directed to a predominantly rural audience' (p. 63). He points to the use of various rural metaphors in the letter (he mentions 1.22-24, 2.25 and 5.2-4) and to the likelihood that *paroikoi*, 'resident aliens' (see below), would be 'numbered among the rural population' (p. 48). However, these arguments do not carry sufficient weight to convince. One of the major impacts of Roman rule was the establishment of a patchwork of cities throughout central Asia Minor (see Mitchell 1993, I: 80-99). And Steven Bechtler (1998: 67) has rightly pointed out that the supposedly rural metaphors could just as well be used by urban authors for urbanized audiences, and has noted that many of the images in the letter are not especially rural. Deductions drawn from the identification of the readers as *paroikoi* depend upon Elliott's questionable argument that this label denotes their socio-political status (see below). Moreover, the description of the slaves as *oiketai* - specifically *household*-slaves - might suggest an urban context, as opposed to the large gangs of slaves working on rural estates. In any case, the distinction between town and country is different in the ancient world than in the modern West. Many of those living in cities (much smaller, of course, than our cities) worked in agriculture or agriculturally-related occupations. Overall, we have to concede that the letter really gives us no strong indications as to the urban versus rural location of its readers. Pliny, once again, makes a relevant comment when he remarks that Christianity has spread through 'not only the towns, but villages and rural districts too' (*Letters* 10.96).

One specific description of the readers of 1 Peter has been subject to considerable discussion in recent scholarship, namely their being labelled as *paroikoi kai parepidēmoi*, 'aliens and exiles' (2.11, NRSV; cf. also 1.1; 1.17). Traditionally, this language has often been taken to depict the Christians as strangers on this earth, a pilgrim people whose home is in heaven. As such it has been taken to have a primarily spiritual and cosmological sense: Christians are not at home in the world because they belong to another world (cf. Heb. 11.13-16; 13.14). This reading of the readers' identity was sharply challenged in John Elliott's important book *A Home for the Homeless* (1981). Elliott explored the meaning of the terms *paroikos* and *parepidēmos* in Greco-Roman and Jewish literature, concluding that *paroikos* refers to an alien permanently residing in an area, while *parepidē-mos* refers to a temporary resident. Elliott argued that the recipients of 1 Peter were literally 'an admixture of perman-ent and temporary strangers and aliens, some of whom are residing permanently and others of whom are living tempor-arily in the five regions or four provinces of Asia Minor' (1981: 47). What this means is that their status as 'aliens and strangers' is a socio-political identity rather than a spiritual one, and an identity which they possessed *prior to*, as well as after, their conversion (pp. 48-49). Elliott's fundamental point is that the alienation and estrangement which characterizes the readers of this letter should be seen as a *sociological* categorization, reflecting the distinction and tension between the members of the Christian communities and those among whom they lived (pp. 42-44).

In his argument that the designation of the readers as *paroikoi* and *parepidēmoi* indicates their social experience, and reflects their state of tension and dislocation from the world around them, Elliott has made an important and compelling point. However, most scholars have remained unconvinced by his argument that these labels indicate the socio-political identity of the addressees. First, it should be noted that the term *paroikos* in Greco-Roman usage primarily indicates a non-citizen, who may or may not be a non-native in the region (Bechtler 1998: 71-74). More crucial, though, is the question as to whether this denotes the addressees' literal, socio-political identity. One indication that it may not is the fact that the recipients can be addressed as *paroikoi kai parepidēmoi* ('aliens and strangers'), despite the fact that the words technically refer to two different categories of person.

Furthermore, they can be addressed, as a group, as *parepidēmoi* (1.1) and as a people who live out a *paroikia*, a 'time of temporary residence' (1.17). This suggests that the words are being used in a more figurative, less precise, sense. Furthermore, the combination of the two terms in 2.11, together with the link with election and diaspora in 1.1, indicate that the background to the use of these terms in 1 Peter is primarily the Jewish scriptures, specifically the LXX. In Gen. 23.4 Abraham, addressing the Hittites among whom he lives, describes himself as 'a stranger [*paroikos*] and an alien [*parepidēmos*] residing among you' (NRSV). This phrase, in which the two crucial words are linked as in 1 Pet. 2.11, recurs a number of times in the Jewish scriptures, where its sense seems to become in some sense spiritualized, as a characterization of the Israelites' existence with God (see Lev. 25.23; 1 Chron. 29.15; Ps. 39.12). This does not mean that it thereby loses any social dimension, but it does suggest that in 1 Peter too the terms are used to evoke something of the dislocation of God's people from the world. (Note, too, that their promised inheritance is described as 'kept in heaven' [1.4].) This therefore suggests that the terms are used to describe the identity of this people as God's people, who, *through their conversion*, have become alienated from the world.

The terms *paroikos* and *parepidēmos* cannot then tell us anything about the socio-political status of the recipients of 1 Peter, since they are used in a more figurative way to describe the estrangement and distance from the world which has been created by conversion to the Christian way of life. However, this sense of dislocation from the world is relevant to consider when we explore the readers' experience as it is depicted in the letter, and specifically their experience of suffering.

Their Experience of Suffering

One thing is clear in the depiction of the letter's recipients: they are experiencing suffering. From the opening thanksgiving (1.6) to the closing section of the letter (5.9-10) this suffering is a prominent theme, a *Leitmotif*, of the text. It is variously described as 'various kinds of trials' (1.6), 'suffering for the sake of righteousness' (3.14), a 'fiery trial' (4.12), and 'sharing the sufferings of Christ' (4.13).

What is somewhat more difficult, but equally important, is to try to understand what kind of suffering is in view here, and what its causes and consequences were. The letter gives us some clues, but we also need to consider if and how this correlates with other evidence, notably from Roman writers who mention Christianity.

The letter mentions some specific scenarios in which Christians might be made to suffer. One such scenario concerns slaves, especially those who have cruel masters (2.18-20). It is also likely, though this is not made explicit in the text, that wives who were married to non-Christian husbands were in a particularly difficult situation (they were conventionally expected to follow the religion of the head of the household; cf. Plutarch, *Moralia* 140D; 1 Pet. 3.1-6). More generally, a number of texts in the letter indicate that Christians were being slandered and criticized by those amongst whom they lived, who regarded them, apparently, as wicked (2.12; 3.14-17; 4.14-16). Finally, the letter indicates that, while the intensity of the suffering and hostility may come as a shock (4.12), similar experiences are shared by Christians throughout the world – so this is no merely local aberration (5.9). Indeed, it is clear from the New Testament and other early Christian literature that suffering due to the negative reactions of those among whom they lived was a common, though not universal, experience of the first Christians. Persecution was not only experienced by leading figures (cf. 1 Thess. 2.2) but also by converts in the churches (e.g., 1 Thess. 1.6; 2.14; 3.3-4; Phil. 1.27-29; Rev. 2.3, 10, 13).

Suffering was expected as an inevitable part of the end-times
(Mk 13.9-13). Whether informal or judicial, hostility could
reach the point where it led to physical punishment or even
death: Stephen was stoned (Acts 7.58; cf. also Acts 14.5, 19);
James was killed by Herod (Acts 12.2); Paul suffered
imprisonment (Phil. 1.7-14; Phlm), Roman and Jewish pun-
ishments (2 Cor. 11.25), and finally execution (cf. 2 Tim. 4.6-
8); a good many, probably including Peter and Paul, were
killed by Nero in 64–65 CE (Tacitus, *Annals* 15.44; *1 Clement*
5.1-7) and, in the decades following, by governors such as
Pliny (*Letters* 10.96-97).

As many recent scholars have pointed out, the situation
depicted in 1 Peter looks like a situation in which Christians
are suffering verbal hostility and ridicule from their neighbours, who react negatively to this new faith and to those
who convert to it. In a recent study of the church at Philippi,
Peter Oakes has given an imaginative but well-informed and
persuasive sketch of how and why such suffering might take
place. Although Oakes's study is not specifically related to
Asia Minor or to 1 Peter, the factors he sees as contributing to
Christian suffering would be equally pertinent here too.
Oakes imagines the situation of a family, Simias, Ianthe, three
children, an elderly grandmother and a slave-girl, who run a
small bakery business; people at the kind of socio-economic
level that would not have been untypical for the early
Christians. Oakes describes how they may have ceased to
participate in the funerary meals of their burial club, removed
a shrine to a popular deity from their shop, and so on, and
considers how these acts may have led to their social
ostracism and physical and economic suffering. Oakes
particularly stresses how economic hardship may have
resulted, for example, from the refusal of other bakers to
continue sharing oven-space, or the loss of flour suppliers or
major customers. He continues:

> Things became worse as word went round that the family
> were members of a strange, subversive, Jewish organiza-

tion. Some people challenged Simias and Ianthe over this and they responded by seeking to persuade them to join the organization and join in the dishonouring of the gods. The daughter of one of the other bakers was actually persuaded. Her father came round in a rage, along with three friends. They beat up Simias and started breaking up the shop. Neighbours, worried that a fire might start, ran to the magistrates. Simias and the other baker were taken off to answer for the disturbance. The magistrates had seen one or two of these troublesome Christians before. Simias received a further beating and a night in prison. Simias was unable to work for a week (Oakes 2001: 90; see pp. 89-91).

As Oakes's sketch indicates, one of the things that would have particularly aroused the hostility of their non-Christian neighbours was the Christians' exclusive devotion to the worship of their God alone, and their refusal to honour the various deities of the Greek and Roman pantheon. Since worshipping the gods was thought to be vital to keeping the peace, and to keeping natural and economic disasters at bay, those who refused to do this could be held responsible for bad things that occurred. Moreover, by withdrawing from such religious and social participation, and meeting in what was held to be a secretive and mysterious manner, Christians were felt to be an 'anti-social' people, who - as the Roman historian Tacitus puts it - became known for their 'hatred of the human race' (*Annals* 15.44). These exclusive aspects of early Christian worship shared much in common with Judaism, of course, but Judaism could claim somewhat greater respect and tolerance as a long-established ancestral religion - whereas Christianity was seen as a new (and wicked) superstition (Tacitus, *Annals* 15.44; Suetonius, *Nero* 16.2; Pliny, *Letters* 10.96). (That said, Jews also suffered considerably due to public prejudice and hostility, as well as in their violent conflicts with Rome.) Soon people began to speculate about what the Christians got up to in their meetings, and, with some snippets of garbled information -

e.g., about the eucharist and their identity as 'brothers and sisters' – accused them of cannibalism, incest, and other such horrors (cf. 1 Pet. 4.15).

However, it is also important to ask whether the suffering of the Christians addressed by 1 Peter went beyond verbal criticism and informal hostility. Could it also include physical suffering, even to death, and was Roman persecution of Christianity also part of the picture? Recent scholarship has tended to move away from the idea that Roman persecution was part of the context for the suffering Christians of 1 Peter. Elliott is a prominent and forceful proponent of this view. He argues that what is depicted in 1 Peter is 'verbal rather than physical abuse' which took the form of 'harassment of Christians by local opponents' (Elliott 1981: 80–81). There is thus no sign in 1 Peter of any confrontation with Rome; instead the letter reflects 'a time of toleration and peaceful coexistence' (p. 86). As he puts it in his recent commentary, '[t]he situation entails intense verbal abuse and incessant maligning and reproach... [But] with no mention in 1 Peter of local arrests, trials, or executions, there is no basis for claiming that at the time of 1 Peter Christianity had been officially proscribed by Rome and that being labeled a Christian implied being charged as a criminal' (Elliott 2000: 794). Or as Steven Bechtler puts it, summarizing his review of recent scholarship: 'Virtually all scholars today agree that the suffering with which 1 Peter is concerned is not due to an Empire-wide persecution of Christians instigated by the emperor; and most describe the situation in terms of social ostracism at the hands of their non-Christian neighbours' (1998: 19).

However, to pose as alternatives informal public hostility and official Roman persecution, as Elliott and others do, is somewhat to misconstrue the situation that pertained, broadly speaking, from the time of Nero until the third-century persecution under Decius (c. 250 CE). In the aftermath of the fire of Rome in 64 CE, as is well known, Nero, seeking to defuse rumours that he had started the fire, hit upon the Christians as scapegoats and had many of them arrested and executed. From this point onwards, or quite soon afterwards, many ancient historians agree, Christianity was effectively illegal, and being a Christian potentially punishable by death. However, this did not mean that the Romans started initiatives to seek out and identify Christians, or enacted any kind of 'official policy' to persecute them. Rather, the procedure by which they acted was the 'accusatorial' process: Christians could be brought to the attention of Roman governors and magistrates by fellow citizens, if they mounted accusations against them.

This could lead to trials in court, and, while those accused might be suspected of other crimes too, the name 'Christian' would be sufficient to convict and render them liable to execution. Although Pliny, in his famous letter (10.96) to the emperor Trajan, proclaims a certain ignorance about how to deal with Christians, there are good arguments for the view that he knew more than he let on, otherwise he would not have been acting as he had been: executing those who confessed the name Christian (or sending them to Rome for trial, if they were citizens). His uncertainty relates mostly to those who admitted they were once Christians, but had since abandoned the faith. Pliny hopes the emperor will agree – as indeed he does – that such people could be released, provided they proved their allegiance to the gods of Rome. Just as public hostility against the Christians probably rested in large part on their secretive exclusiveness and refusal to join in worship of the gods, so too did official Roman objection to the Christians. Their refusal to worship the gods and offer proper devotion to the emperor indicated an intolerable stance of both religious and political rebellion, not least since the peaceable existence of the Roman order, the *pax Romana*, was considered to depend upon sustaining the goodwill of the gods, the *pax deorum*.

Interestingly, Pliny indicates that he has gone somewhat beyond the standard form of the accusatorial process: he has identified some Christians whose names were provided on an anonymous pamphlet. In his brief reply, which generally affirms Pliny's actions regarding the Christians, Trajan mildly reprimands him for this step, which violates the Roman principle that the accuser must publicly name and face their antagonist. Thus Trajan (as later does emperor Hadrian) insists that Christians must not be hunted out, but only dealt with through the process of accusation. This means, of course, that precisely the kind of public hostility and antagonism towards Christians that most rightly see lying behind 1 Peter can lead to Christians being accused and brought to court. And when this happens, if they acknowledge the name 'Christian', they are liable to punishment and execution. In other words, it was a combination of public *and* imperial hostility that resulted in formal actions against Christians.

So the situation of the readers addressed by 1 Peter is one of suffering, suffering that results from hostility towards them at both the informal and the imperial level. This suffering will often have been felt at the level of antagonism, slander and social ostracism from those amongst whom they lived – a form of suffering, as Oakes shows, that could well have practical, physical and economic consequences, as well as emotional and social ones. But for some Christians, who were unlucky enough to be named and accused before the Roman magistrates, their suffering could also entail their trial and execution as criminals. In both cases, the reasons for hostility against the Christians were somewhat similar, centring around their refusal to worship the Roman gods and to revere the emperor. In so doing, they threatened the peaceable existence of society and the established order of the empire. Religious and political factors are here inextricably combined. We shall explore the dynamics of this suffering further, in Chapter 5, when we consider the ways in which 1 Peter addresses this difficult situation and advises the recipients of the letter about how to live in a hostile world, and specifically in the Roman empire. Before that, however, we turn to consider positively how 1 Peter draws on the resources of Jewish scripture to construct a positive sense of Christian identity for the suffering recipients of the letter.

Further Reading

Elliott's influential monograph, *A Home for the Homeless* (1981), arguing (among other things) that the recipients of 1 Peter were literally non-native aliens and strangers is listed, along with the commentaries of Elliott (2000) and Jobes (2005), at the end of Chapter 1. For critical reactions, and further discussion of the identity of the addressees, see:

Bechtler, Steven R., *Following in His Steps: Suffering, Community, and Christology in 1 Peter* (SBLDS, 162; Atlanta, GA: Scholars Press, 1998).

Feldmeier, Reinhard, *Die Christen als Fremde* (WUNT, 64; Tübingen: Mohr Siebeck, 1992).

Feldmeier, Reinhard, 'The "Nation" of Strangers: Social Contempt and its Theological Interpretations in Ancient Judaism and Early Christianity', in M.G. Brett (ed.), *Ethnicity and the Bible* (Leiden: Brill, 1996), 240-70.

Seland, Torrey, *Strangers in the Night: Philonic Perspectives on Christian Identity in 1 Peter* (Biblical Interpretation Series, 76; Leiden: Brill, 2005).

The best and most comprehensive work on Asia Minor in the Roman period is:

Mitchell, Stephen, *Anatolia: Land, Men, and Gods in Asia Minor, Volume I: The Celts and the Impact of Roman Rule; Volume II: The Rise of the Church* (Oxford: Clarendon, 1993).

On Jewish communities in Asia Minor see:

Trebilco, Paul R., *Jewish Communities in Asia Minor* (SNTSMS, 69; Cambridge: Cambridge University Press, 1991).

On the 'elders' in early Christianity, see:

> Campbell, R. Alastair, *The Elders: Seniority within Earliest Christianity* (SNTW; Edinburgh: T&T Clark, 1994).

On the suffering and persecution of the early Christians, see:

> Frend, William H.C., 'Martyrdom and Political Oppression', in Philip F. Esler (ed.), *The Early Christian World* (London and New York: Routledge, 2000), 815-39.

> Oakes, Peter, *Philippians: From People to Letter* (SNTSMS, 110; Cambridge: Cambridge University Press, 2001).

> Ste Croix, G.E.M. de, 'Why Were the Early Christians Persecuted?' *Past and Present* 26 (1963), 6-38.

> Sordi, Marta, *The Christians and the Roman Empire* (London: Routledge, 1994).

> Vos, Craig S. de, 'Popular Graeco-Roman Responses to Christianity', in P.F. Esler (ed.), *The Early Christian World* (London and New York: Routledge, 2000), II, 869-89.

For discussion of Pliny's letter, and specifically arguments that Roman proscription of Christianity predates the time of Pliny and that Pliny knows more about the legal basis for condemning Christians than his letter might seem to imply, see:

> Horrell, David G., 'The Label *Christianos*: 1 Pet. 4.16 and the Formation of Christian Identity', *Journal of Biblical Literature* 126 (2007), 361-81 [=2007a].

> Molthagen, Joachim, 'Die Lage der Christen im römischen Reich nach dem 1. Petrusbrief: Zum Problem einer Domitianischen Verfolgung', *Historia* 44 (1995), 422-58.

> Molthagen, Joachim, ' "Cognitionibus de Christianis interfui numquam." Das Nichtwissen des Plinius und die Anfänge der Christenprozesse', *Zeitschrift für Theologie und Gemeinde* 9 (2004), 112-40.

4

JEWISH SCRIPTURES AND CHRISTIAN IDENTITY

We have already seen something of the way in which 1 Peter makes extensive use of the Jewish scriptures as one of the most important traditions from which the letter's content is constructed (see Chapter 2). In this chapter we shall be probing certain aspects of this central characteristic of the letter further. In particular, we shall be interested in the ways in which the author draws upon the Jewish scriptures in order to describe who Christ is, how he has acted and what he has achieved, and also to describe the character and identity of Christians. In other words, one of the things the author is doing in drawing on the Jewish scriptures is constructing a sense of 'Christian' identity. This raises certain theological and ethical questions, as we shall see, particularly concerning what the author thus implies about the continuing existence of the Jews.

A Christological Hermeneutic: 1.10-12

In the opening thanksgiving of the letter (1.3-12), the author proclaims the blessedness of God on account of the glorious salvation God has prepared for believers. Despite their trials, they can rejoice as they anticipate the goal of their faith: salvation (1.9). At this point, the author looks back to the prophets of the Hebrew scriptures,.describing them as having carefully inquired into this salvation and having prophesied concerning 'the grace that was to be yours' (1.10). As they sought to know to whom and to what period of time their prophecies pointed (the Greek phrase here, it should be

noted, is compact and open to various interpretations), 'the
spirit of Christ' made it clear to them, 'witnessing in advance
to the sufferings destined for Christ and the subsequent
glories' (1.11). Thus it was revealed to the prophets of old
that their ministry – the word and message they proclaimed –
was for 'your sake' (1.12): the author 'identifies what was
foreknown by the prophets to be the very things that have
now been preached to his readers through those who
evangelized them' (Jobes 2005: 103).

This short passage is interesting and important in various
respects. The author depicts the concern of the Jewish
prophets as looking forward, trying to ascertain the time and
circumstances when God's salvation would be realized, when
their eschatological visions would come to pass, when the
Messiah would appear. A concern to determine when the
eschatological future would arrive is hardly an issue for most
of the prophets of the Hebrew Bible. But it does become
prominent in later Jewish literature, from the second century
BCE onwards (e.g. Dan. 9.1-27; 12.6-13; 4 Ezra 4.33-46;
1QpHab 7.1-13). The author of 1 Peter shares with such
Jewish literature the belief that the focus of the ancient
prophecies was indeed the 'end-time', and, like those Jews
whose expectations are reflected in the Qumran literature,
saw that end-time as drawing very near (1.5-7; 4.7, 17; cf. p.
33 above).

Where 1 Peter diverges from Jewish interpretative practice,
of course, is in his claim that the ancient Jewish prophets
were informed by 'the spirit of Christ' – a striking phrase, rare
in the NT (Rom. 8.9; cf. Acts 16.7; Gal. 4.6; Phil. 1.19) – and
that what they foresaw was the suffering and glory destined
for Christ (*Christos* means anointed one, or Messiah). In
effect, this constitutes a claim that the true *subject* of biblical
prophecy – and, by extension, of the Jewish scriptures as a
whole – is Christ, and that the fulfilment of what is said by the
prophets is found in the Christian gospel and is appropriated
by Christian believers. The author of 1 Peter shares with other
early Christians the conviction that the coming of Christ

marked the beginning of the end-times, the final act in God's drama of salvation (1.20; cf. 1 Cor. 10.11; Heb. 1.2).

What we find in 1.10-12 then, as William Schutter (1989: 100-23) and Paul Achtemeier (1999: 144-47) have pointed out, is a hermeneutical key – a text that indicates how and why the author reads the Jewish scriptures from a Christian perspective, interpreting them as pointing to Christ and fulfilled in Christ. Such a view of scripture is, of course, broadly shared by other early Christian writers (cf. Mk 1.1-8; Lk. 24.25-32; Rom. 15.4; 1 Cor. 10.1-11; Heb. 10.1-22; etc.). But it is expressed here in a striking and particular way, and helps us to appreciate the author's use of scripture elsewhere in the letter.

The Suffering Christ as Example: 2.21-25

Given this explicitly Christian-messianic view of scriptural prophecy, it is no surprise that the author can draw heavily on Isaiah's suffering servant material (Isa. 52.13–53.12, esp. 53.3-12) to describe the sufferings of Christ (2.21-25). Isaiah 53 has become well known and well established as a key biblical prophecy in which Christians see a prefiguring of the vicarious sufferings of Christ. It is therefore worthwhile to point out that explicit use of Isaiah's suffering servant material is surprisingly restricted elsewhere in the NT, compared with its extensive and explicit use here in 1 Peter. Making this very point, Paul Achtemeier mentions Mt. 8.17, Mk 10.45, Lk. 22.37, Acts 8.32-33 and Rom. 4.25 as texts where Isaiah 53 is cited or echoed, but notes that even in the fullest such citation, Acts 8.32-33, where Isaiah 53 is clearly 'understood to refer to Jesus, it receives no further explication. When Luke does come to describe the Passion, he ignores the Isaianic material' (Achtemeier 1999: 147). This makes 1 Pet. 2.21-25 especially important as the most extensive and explicit early Christian interpretation of this influential prophetic text. Indeed, as Karen Jobes remarks, 'it is only here in the NT that Christ's passion is discussed in

terms of Isaiah's prophecy of the Suffering Servant' (Jobes
2005: 192). She lists Mt. 8.17, Lk. 22.37, Jn 12.38, Acts 8.32-
33, Rom. 10.16 and 15.21 as the 'six direct quotations of
Isaiah 53 in the NT', noting (somewhat questionably, in my
view) that 'only two of them are used in reference to Jesus'.
Jobes goes on to note, like Achtemeier, that Acts 8.32-35 is,
aside from 1 Peter 2, 'the closest Christological use of Isaiah
53...but there is no actual exposition in that passage of the
specific elements of Isaiah 53 as they relate to Jesus' (pp.
192-93). Matthew, Luke–Acts, and John seem to assume
some Christological significance to Isaiah's servant material,
but they do not spell it out. Jobes therefore rightly concludes:
'We are thus indebted to the apostle Peter alone [or to the
author of 1 Peter, if one doubts that Peter was himself the
writer] for his distinctive Christological use of the Suffering
Servant passage to interpret the significance of the suffering
and death of Jesus' (p. 193).

The extent of the relationship with the text of Isaiah may
be seen from the table below (precise parallels are under-
lined; less precise overlaps are indicated by dotted underlin-
ing; parts of the Isaiah text with possible echoes in 1 Peter 2
are included in italics):

Use of Isaiah 53 in 1 Peter 2.21-25

1 Peter 2.21-25	Isaiah 53 (LXX)
21 For to this you were called, because Christ also suffered for you, leaving you an example, so that you might follow in his steps	
22 who committed no sin, nor was any deceit found in his mouth,	he committed no lawlessness, nor was any deceit found in his mouth (v. 9)
23 who, when insulted, did not reply with insults, when he suffered, did not threaten, but handed himself over to the one who judges justly;	*When he was mistreated, he did not open his mouth* (v. 7) *It was the Lord's will to crush him...* (v. 10) ...was handed over (v. 12, twice)

24 who himself bore our sins in his body on the tree, so that dying to sins we might live for righteousness, by whose wounds you are healed. 25 For you were like sheep going astray, but now you have returned to the shepherd and guardian of your souls.

he bears our sins (v. 4)// and himself bore the sins of many (v. 12)// he himself will bear their sins (v. 11) by his wounds we are healed (v. 5) like sheep we were going astray (v. 6).

As we have already seen (see Chapter 2), this section of 1 Peter may possibly draw on traditional Christian credal material about Christ. If that is so - and such arguments inevitably remain rather speculative - then that earlier material also drew on Isaiah 53 to express beliefs about what Christ had done. Certainly, Acts 8.32-35 indicates that the use of Isaiah 53 to describe the sufferings of Christ had become established in early Christian thought by the time Luke wrote; it has been argued that the identification of Jesus with the 'suffering servant' goes back to Jesus himself, who understood his own identity and mission in such terms, though this particular proposal has been sharply criticized (see Hooker 1959). Whether and to what extent the author of 1 Peter was being innovative in applying the Isaianic servant imagery to Jesus depends therefore on questions as to how far back this identification goes, and also, of course, on the dating of 1 Peter (see Chapter 1) compared with other NT documents. It seems likely that the author of 1 Peter was not the first to find Christological significance in Isaiah's suffering servant material. He does, however, provide our earliest exposition using Isaiah's text to depict the sufferings of Christ - perhaps drawing on early Christian tradition in doing so. If it is the case that the author is drawing on tradition, then he himself is clearly not being innovative in depicting Christ as the suffering servant of Isaiah, but he still presents our only explicit and developed NT record of this tradition, which is glimpsed and assumed elsewhere.

In addition to its significance as an example of the Christological use of the Jewish scriptures, this text is important for the understanding of 1 Peter's message, its theology and ethics. Jobes describes 1 Pet. 2.21-25 as 'the heart of 1 Peter's Christology' (Jobes 2005: 192). As we have seen, the text depicts Christ as the innocent victim, who did not return abuse with abuse or violence with violence, but suffered quietly, entrusting himself to God (probably the implied 'one who judges justly', v. 23). This suffering was redemptive, a vicarious act in which Christ bore the sins of others on the cross (*xulon*, 'wood/tree', used of the cross in Acts 5.30, 10.39, 13.29; cf. Gal. 3.13), bringing them healing and the possibility of a new life of righteousness.

More than this, Christ's conduct is presented as an example, a model set out 'so that you may follow in his steps' (2.21; cf. 4.1). We have already seen how the issue of suffering is central to the themes and concerns of 1 Peter. Here we see how Christ is presented as the pattern for suffering Christians to follow. It is important, though, to notice the context in which this key Christological passage appears. It forms part of the section addressed to slaves (2.18-25) who may suffer unjustly at the hand of cruel masters. These household slaves (*oiketai*) in particular are encouraged to bear such suffering while continuing to do good, since such conduct is creditable in God's sight (2.19-20). This pattern of life is their calling, for which Christ is the example to follow (2.21).

This teaching does not only apply to slaves, however. As Elliott has pointed out, 'what is said here to household servants is true for the suffering community as a whole' (Elliott 2000: 523). Indeed, Elliott suggests, in the context of his argument that the 'household of God' is the central image of the church in 1 Peter, 'the household slaves are paradigmatic for the household membership as a whole' (1981: 206). All Christians addressed by 1 Peter are urged to be steadfast in doing good, not to return slander for slander, and to endure suffering while entrusting themselves to God (4.19) and hoping firmly in their promised salvation (1.3-9). Indeed, these themes are also reiterated in the most extensive scriptural quotation in 1 Peter, at 3.10-12 (quoting Ps. 34.12-16 [LXX 33.13-17]), a quotation which may be seen as pivotal to the whole letter (Woan 2004). Here, too, the message is that those who seek life must keep away from evil and do good, confident that the Lord watches over the righteous.

There is, of course, more to say about the Christology of 1 Peter. As we have already seen in Chapter 2, the letter also refers to Christ as chosen before the foundation of the world (1.20) and as now seated in power at God's right hand (3.22). There are no clear or explicit descriptions of Christ as God, or as divine (cf. Phil. 2.6; Col. 1.19; 2.9; Tit. 2.13), but Christ is evidently seen as having existed before his birth and, indeed, as having been present, by his spirit, with the prophets of old (1.11). The whole 'story' of Christ – from before the world began, through his appearance, suffering, death and resurrection, to victory over opposing powers and exaltation in heaven – is reflected in 1 Peter, in a way comparable to the compact credal summary in 1 Tim. 3.16. But the main focus is on his suffering, which is the most relevant issue for the letter's recipients. Other texts in the letter also use biblical imagery to describe his death and its salvific effect: 'sprinkling with his blood' (1.2); 'redeemed…by the precious blood of Christ, like that of a lamb without fault or flaw' (1.18-19). Here the particular imagery is drawn from the Jewish sacrificial system: Exod. 24.3-9 records the covenant sacrifices made by Moses at Sinai, who 'took the blood and threw it on the people' (v. 8). (This sacrificial interpretation of Christ's death, drawing on Exod. 24.3-9, is more extensively developed in Heb. 9.11-27.) Numbers 19 describes the sprinkling of blood, ashes and water for the purpose of purification. The specific image of the lamb is found in Isa. 53.7; but the dominant image in the background of 1.19 is probably that of the Passover lamb, which, like other sacrifices, had to be without blemish (see Exod. 12.5; Lev. 22.17-25; 1 Cor. 5.7; Heb. 9.14). The special significance of 2.21-25, apart from its sheer length, is that here the depiction of Christ's redemptive suffering combines theology and ethics in a way that is close to the heart of the letter's concerns: this is the pattern for Christian discipleship and specifically for Christians who suffer (see Elliott 1985).

Christ and the Church: 2.4-10

In 2.4-10, the opening of which is closely linked to 2.3, we find one of the richest and most important texts in the epistle, the climax of the first major section of the letter-body. It is an intricately constructed text, into which a number of biblical texts are woven: it is aptly described by Richard Bauckham (1988: 310) as 'a particularly complex and studied piece of exegesis'. Verses 4-5 serve as an introduction to the exposition that follows, summarizing its key themes. But the primary sources of these ideas are in the texts quoted and echoed in vv. 6-10; in other words, these biblical texts generate the ideas that are then summarized in the introduction to the section, rather than the other way round, in which case the texts would serve only to illustrate or prove the points already made (see Elliott 1966: 48; Bauckham 1988: 310-11). The way in which these texts are quoted and interpreted bears some similarity with Jewish midrash, and specifically the *pesharim* ('interpretations') from Qumran (on Isaiah, Hosea, other prophets, and the Psalms) in which a text is quoted and then its interpretation given, as in the following example:

> 'And those who hope in YHWH will inherit the land' [Ps. 37.9]. Its interpretation: they are the congregation of his elect who carry out his will. 'A short while yet and the wicked will no longer exist [...] I will stare at his place and he will no longer be there' [Ps. 37.10]. Its interpretation concerns all the evil at the end of the forty years, for they

shall be devoured and upon the earth no wicked person will be found (4Q171 [Psalms Pesher[a]] 2.4-8, trans. García Martínez).

As is made clear in the summarizing introduction in vv. 4-5, there are two key themes in this section: Jesus as the precious and elect stone, and the Church, comprised of 'living stones', as the elect and holy people of God (see also Elliott 1966). In vv. 6-8 a series of three texts, linked together by the catch-word 'stone' (*lithos*), which occurs in them all, are quoted and interpreted. (The technique of linking texts together through common catch-words or topics is also paralleled in Jewish exegetical practice.) The texts and their interpretative comments may be set out as follows (following the NRSV translation):

Introductory formula: For it stands in scripture:

First quotation: 'See, I am laying in Zion a stone, a cornerstone chosen and precious; and whoever believes in him will not be put to shame.' (Isa. 28.16 LXX)

Interpretative comment applying the text to the readers and their opponents: To you then who believe, he is precious; but for those who do not believe,

Second quotation: 'The stone that the builders rejected has become the very head of the corner,' (Ps. 118.22 [117.22 LXX])

Third quotation: and 'A stone of stumbling, and a rock of offense.' (Isa. 8.14)

Interpretative comment: They stumble because they disobey the word, as they were destined to do.

As in 2.21-25, here too texts from the Jewish scriptures are interpreted messianically, that is, as applying to Christ. As is probably true of the use of Isaiah 53 in 2.21-25, though again depending to some extent on when one dates 1 Peter relative to other NT texts, the author of 1 Peter is not being innovative in seeing messianic significance in these particular texts. Indeed, the 'stone' texts cited here are already cited as messianic texts elsewhere in the NT (Mk 12.10-11 and par.; Rom. 9.32-33; cf. Acts 4.11). There are also some parallels in the use of such imagery to express eschatological expectations about the community at Qumran (see pp. 33-4 above). But what the author of 1 Peter does do - uniquely in the NT - is to draw all three of these texts together and weave them into his own depiction of Christ's identity and fate, which also serves as a pattern for the believer's life in the world.

Indeed, the final section of this piece of text turns to focus on the Christians themselves, and on their identity as the people of God. Here again a number of texts from the Jewish scriptures are cited, this time linked together by the catchword 'people' (*laos*). Unlike in vv. 6-8, however, in vv. 9-10 these texts (italicized below) are woven more thoroughly into a single patchwork of phrases (quoted again from the NRSV):

> But you are a *chosen race* (Isa. 43.20), *a royal priesthood, a holy nation* (Exod. 19.6), *God's own people*, in order that *you may proclaim the mighty acts of him* (Isa. 43.21) who called you out of darkness into his marvelous light. Once you were *not a people*, but now you are *God's people*; once you had *not received mercy*, but now *you have received mercy* (Hos. 2.23 [2.25 LXX]; cf. 1.6, 9, 10 [2.1 LXX]).

One of the striking things about this collection of phrases is the way in which it draws on the Jewish scriptures, indeed on some of the central identity designations of Israel ('chosen race', 'holy people', 'God's people', etc.), to describe the identity of the mainly Gentile recipients of the letter (see Chapter 3 above). Just as the letter opened with a designation of the readers in thoroughly Jewish terms - as the elect strangers of the Diaspora (1.1; see Chapter 3) - so here, too, the positive depiction of their glorious new status is made in terms drawn from the heritage of Judaism.

The description of the readers as 'elect' (cf. also 1.1) adopts a label for God's people in the Jewish scriptures widely used in early Christian literature (e.g., Deut. 4.37; 7.6-8; Ps. 78.68; 135.4; Isa. 41.8-9; 44.1; Mk 13.20, 22, 27; Rom. 8.33; Col. 3.12; 2 Tim. 2.10; Tit. 1.1; Rev. 17.14). As Peter Richardson notes (1969: 172 n. 8), 1 Pet. 2.9 is the only place in the NT where the term *genos* (meaning race, family, or tribe) is applied to the Church, though it is common as a term to describe the people of Israel in the Jewish scriptures (e.g. LXX Exod. 1.9; Josh. 4.14; Dan. 1.6) and becomes common later, notably in the description of Christians as a 'third race', alongside Jews and Gentiles. The phrase 'holy people' (*ethnos hagion*) is not often found as such (but see Exod. 19.6; 23.22 [LXX]; Wis. 17.2), but the theme of Israel's call to be holy is common, especially in the book of Leviticus (e.g., Lev. 11.44-45; 19.2; 20.7, 26; cf. 1 Pet. 1.16). Similarly, the phrase 'people of God' (*laos theou*) is not itself a precisely established label, but the description of the people as the *laos* is very common, and they are often specifically denoted as 'your people', or 'my people', where God (*theos*) is the one to whom they belong (e.g. Exod. 33.16; 2 Sam. 7.23; 1 Kgs 8.43; Isa. 64.8).

So the people addressed by the author of 1 Peter are, in effect, given the identity of the people of Israel, as the author seeks to give them hope and assurance in their faith and their salvation. This adoption of Jewish identity-terms to describe the Christian movement is, of course, by no means unique to 1 Peter. On the contrary, it is characteristic, in various ways, of the NT as a whole and relates to the whole complex process by which Christianity, which began as an inner-Jewish movement, eventually became something distinct from Judaism, and claimed to represent the 'true' fulfilment of Judaism's heritage. Jewish scripture and tradition were the main reservoirs from which the early Christians drew in order to describe what they believed God had done in Christ, and what they had thus become. Paul, for example, refers to believers in Christ as 'sons of Abraham' (Gal. 3.7, 29), the true 'circumcision' (Phil. 3.3; cf. Rom. 2.25-29), children of the Jerusalem above (Gal. 4.26), in contrast with 'the present

Jerusalem and her children' (Gal. 4.25). He can refer to 'the
Israel according to the flesh' (1 Cor. 10.18), which stands in
implicit contrast with a new Israel, or a redefined Israel,
according to the Spirit or the promise (cf. Rom. 9.7-8; Gal.
4.21-31).

As in other aspects of 1 Peter we have already mentioned –
the use of Isaiah 53, or the messianic interpretation of the
stone texts – it is not that the author of 1 Peter does
something unique or unprecedented in applying Jewish self-
descriptions to the Christian churches. Rather, as indeed with
the other examples mentioned above, what 1 Peter provides
is a particularly striking and developed example of this facet
of early Christian theology. As Richardson notes, the 'trans-
positions' of Jewish attributes and titles to the Church 'reach
a climax within the New Testament in [1 Peter] 2.1-10', a text
which represents 'a conscious attempt...to appropriate the
Ehrentitel Israels [the honorific titles of Israel] for the new
people of God' (1969: 172-73). Verses 9–10 in particular
present a rich mixture of biblical phrases to describe the
identity of those to whom the letter is addressed. More
broadly, Paul Achtemeier suggests that 'Israel as a totality has
become for this letter the controlling metaphor in terms of
which its theology is expressed' (Achtemeier 1996: 69). One
can well understand why some early Christian writers,
including Eusebius, took 1 Peter to be addressed to Jewish
Christians (see Chapter 3 above).

What the author of 1 Peter is doing, then, is using the
resources of Jewish scripture and identity to give a positive
sense of identity to the recipients of the letter, who are hard-
pressed due to their negative experience of hostility and
suffering, and the criticism and slander they receive from
their neighbours. In social-psychological terms, the author is
pursuing a certain strategy to reverse this negative valuation
of the believers' identity. While those around them may
condemn them as evildoers, and criticize their faith and
conduct, the author insists that they have a glorious and
highly valued identity as God's special people.

What is more, 1 Peter applies these (Jewish) labels to the early Christian converts without giving any explicit indication that these texts and titles also belong to the ethnic and historic people of Israel, the Jews. The letter is simply silent about the question of 'unconverted' Israel – the question about which Paul agonizes in the long and complex argument of Romans 9-11. Achtemeier comments: 'In 1 Peter the language and hence the reality of Israel pass *without remainder* into the language and hence the reality of the new people of God' (Achtemeier 1996: 69, my emphasis; see further pp. 67-73). Or, as Achtemeier puts it elsewhere, the author of 1 Peter 'has...appropriated *without remainder* the language of Israel for the church' (Achtemeier 1999: 142, my emphasis). Does this imply, as Richardson suggests, that '[t]he Church has taken over the inheritance...of Israel' (1969: 174)?

This adoption – or, should we say, 'taking over'? – of the scriptures and identity of Israel therefore raises challenging historical, theological and ethical questions which rapidly connect with the contemporary issue of the relationship and understanding between Christianity and Judaism. Again the issue is by no means unique to 1 Peter, but it is an important consideration for contemporary interpreters of the New Testament. We shall return to it in Chapter 6, when we consider some of the issues facing today's readers of 1 Peter.

Further Reading

On the use of Jewish scripture in 1 Peter, relevant works by Schutter and Woan have already been mentioned in the suggestions for further reading at the end of Chapter 2. For the commentaries of Achtemeier (1996), Elliott (2000), and Jobes (2005), and the book by Elliott (1981), see Chapter 1. For an assessment of the influence of Isaiah 53 (and the 'servant songs') on Jesus and the early church, and the argument that Jesus did not see himself as the 'suffering servant', see:

Hooker, Morna D., *Jesus and the Servant* (London: SPCK, 1959).

For more recent discussion, see:

Bellinger, William H. and Farmer, William R. (eds), *Jesus and the Suffering Servant: Isaiah 53 and Christian Origins* (Harrisburg, PA: Trinity Press International, 1998).

An assessment of the use of Isaiah in 1 Peter is presented in:

Moyise, Steve, 'Isaiah in 1 Peter', in Steve Moyise and Maarten J.J. Menken (eds), *Isaiah in the New Testament* (London and New York: T&T Clark, 2005), 175–88.

On the use of the Jewish scriptures in 2.4-10, see:

Bauckham, Richard J., 'James, 1 and 2 Peter, Jude', in Don A. Carson and Hugh G.M. Williamson (eds), *It is Written: Scripture Citing Scripture* (Cambridge: Cambridge University Press, 1988), 303–17.

Elliott, John H., *The Elect and the Holy: An Exegetical Examination of 1 Peter 2.4-10 and the Phrase* Basileion Hierateuma (NovTSup, 12; Leiden: Brill, 1966).

An accessible introduction to the way in which the Jewish scriptures are used in the New Testament is provided in:

Moyise, Steve, *The Old Testament in the New: An Introduction* (London and New York: T&T Clark, 2001).

On the Christology of 1 Peter, and specifically the ways in which Christ is presented as a pattern for discipleship, see:

Achtemeier, Paul J., 'The Christology of 1 Peter: Some Reflections', in Mark A. Powell and David R. Bauer (eds), *Who Do You Say That I Am? Essays on Christology in Honor of Jack Dean Kingsbury* (Louisville: Westminster John Knox, 1999), 140–54.

Elliott, John H., 'Backward and Forward "In His Steps": Following Jesus from Rome to Raymond and Beyond. The

Tradition, Redaction, and Reception of 1 Peter 2.18-25', in Fernando F. Segovia (ed.), *Discipleship in the New Testament* (Philadelphia: Fortress, 1985), 184-209.

On the use of Israel's identity to describe the church in 1 Peter, in addition to the commentary by Achtemeier and his essay listed above, see:

Richardson, Peter, *Israel in the Apostolic Church* (SNTSMS, 10; Cambridge: Cambridge University Press, 1969).

5

BECOMING CHRISTIAN IN A HOSTILE WORLD

In the previous chapter, our focus was on the ways in which the author of 1 Peter drew upon the Jewish scriptures to describe the achievements of Christ and the identity of the (mostly Gentile) Christians to whom he wrote. One of the broader issues this raised was the relationship of Christianity to Judaism, and what the material in 1 Peter implies about this. In this chapter, by contrast, we will be concerned with the relationship of Christians with the wider world, and specifically the Roman empire. Christianity found its origins in Judaism, and to Judaism it owes its first scriptures, and the basic resources from which its content and identity are formed. But, like Jews, Christians also had to negotiate their place and existence in a wider world that was often hostile to them. Indeed, this issue goes hand in hand with that of the Church's emergence and separation from Judaism, since the more Christians began to be noticed and identified as somewhat distinct, something new, the more directly they had to face hostility and accusation.

Having explored in Chapter 3 the nature of the hostility and suffering experienced by the early Christians addressed by 1 Peter, our task in this chapter is to consider how the letter confronts this experience and encourages and instructs its readers. How does the letter expect its readers to negotiate their existence in a hostile world, and how does it give hope and encouragement to people often slandered and condemned? Does it urge them to quietly conform and obey, in order to stay out of trouble? Or does it urge them to resist the demands to conform, even if suffering is the result? How exactly does the letter position the Church in relation to the world, and specifically the Roman empire?

The Church and the World: The Balch–Elliott Debate

A good way into this discussion is via an important and well-known debate among scholars of 1 Peter. As we noted at the outset of this book, 1 Peter has often been somewhat neglected in NT studies, and has not often been at the centre of debate. One exception to this situation came in the early 1980s, stimulated by the publication in 1981 of two monographs on 1 Peter, which came to contrasting conclusions about the strategy of the letter, particularly concerning the way the Church should relate to the world. These books are David L. Balch's work, *Let Wives Be Submissive*, a revised version of Balch's PhD dissertation presented in 1974, and John H. Elliott's work, *A Home for the Homeless*. Following the publication of these works, the two authors engaged in a debate at the 1982 annual joint meeting of the American Academy of Religion (AAR) and the Society of Biblical Literature (SBL), and the papers they presented were subsequently published in 1986.

The focus of Balch's work was the domestic code in 1 Peter (1 Pet. 2.11-3.12). Balch traced the origins of this type of 'household instruction' material (cf. also Col. 3.18-4.1; Eph. 5.21-6.9) to the Greek 'household management' tradition stemming from Plato and Aristotle. In terms of the function of this material in 1 Peter, Balch saw this as connected with the tensions evident between Christians and their wider society. Such tensions would have been especially prominent in households where some individual members, slaves or wives for example (cf. 1 Pet. 2.18-20; 3.1-6), had converted to Christianity (seen as a suspicious new Eastern cult) without the head of the household, or the household as a whole, having done so. As we noted above (p. 53), the conventional expectation was that household members would follow the patterns of religious observance of the head of the household.

According to Balch, in the domestic code instruction the author of 1 Peter is urging such Christians to lessen criticism of themselves by conforming as closely as possible to the social norms of the time, without compromising their commitment to Christ. In Balch's terms, the code has an *apologetic* purpose, defending Christians against hostile criticism by showing that their pattern of behaviour is what is generally regarded as good and acceptable. In his SBL paper, Balch compares this with the forms of acculturation or assimilation adopted by immigrants and other members of minority cultures, faced with the pressures of living in a dominant culture different from their own. In short, the purpose of 1 Peter, and specifically its domestic code, was to lessen the hostility and antagonism suffered by Christians by urging them to closer conformity to conventional social expectations. The Church, in other words, was to accommodate to the world, to reduce as far as possible the distance and tension between Christians and those around them.

Elliott's work, presenting for the first time a 'sociological' approach to understanding 1 Peter, took a different approach to the letter. We have already discussed one of the key starting points in Elliott's argument (see Chapter 3), namely his proposal that the terms *paroikoi* and *parepidēmoi*, aliens and strangers (cf. 1 Pet. 1.1; 1.17; 2.11), are not used metaphorically but instead indicate the socio-political status of the addressees of 1 Peter. For these estranged and dislocated people, the Church offered a 'home', a place of belonging in which these 'strangers' found a positive and valued identity as God's own people - hence the title of Elliott's book, *A Home for the Homeless*. The strategy of 1 Peter, then, is to foster internal cohesion among the 'brotherhood' (2.17; 5.9), to build a distinctive communal identity and resist external pressures to conform.

In order to understand the character of the Christian communities and their relationship with the wider world, Elliott suggests that a helpful model is that of the religious sect, as depicted by contemporary sociologists of religion,

such as Bryan Wilson. More specifically, drawing on a
typology of sects developed by Wilson, Elliott categorizes
the church depicted in 1 Peter as a 'conversionist sect'. This is
a sect which regards the world as an evil and hostile place,
but which at the same time considers itself to have a
missionary task, to save individuals from this wicked world
through conversion into the sect. Elliott's stress, therefore, is
on the distinction between the Church and the world. In
direct opposition to Balch, he argues that:

> nothing in 1 Peter, including its discussion of household
> duties, indicates an interest in promoting social assimila-
> tion. It was precisely a temptation to assimilate so as to
> avoid further suffering that the letter intended to counter-
> act...the letter affirms the distinctive communal identity
> and seeks to strengthen the solidarity of the Christian
> brotherhood so that it might resist external pressure urging
> cultural conformity and thereby make effective witness to
> the distinctive features of its communal life, its allegiance
> and its hope of salvation (Elliott 1986: 72-73, 78).

The contrast with Balch's conclusions is clear, and leads to a
very different assessment of the Church's relationship with
the world. Where Balch sees assimilation and conformity,
Elliott sees distinctiveness and resistance.

The initial question, of course, is which approach best
captures the dynamics of 1 Peter and best expresses the
letter's view of the ways Christians should relate to the world.
Beyond that, we might want to ask whether other kinds of
approach might enable us to find different ways of describing
and accounting for the diverse material in 1 Peter, to which
both Balch and Elliott draw our attention.

In beginning to assess this debate, and trying to grasp the
social dynamics of the letter itself, it is important to draw
attention to what both Elliott and Balch recognize as
characteristic of 1 Peter, namely that there is some material
that seems to suggest a convergence between what Elliott
calls 'Christian and secular valuations of behavior', while

other material appears to stress the distinctiveness of the Christian community (Elliott 1986: 66). Is it then the case that both Balch and Elliott are right, in that some of the material in 1 Peter fits both of their perspectives? Is there a consistent stance towards the world in the letter? In assessing these arguments, and exploring other perspectives that might also be valuable, we shall look first at various aspects of the letter's teaching on Christian life in the world, before returning to consider what this seems to suggest about 1 Peter's perspective on the world and the empire.

Doing Good and Honouring the Emperor

One of the prominent themes in the instruction 1 Peter gives to its addressees is to 'turn away from evil and do good' (3.11, quoting Ps. 34.14). A number of times in the letter, Christians are warned not to do anything that could justify their being labelled an 'evildoer' (2.12; 4.15; cf. 2.14). Sometimes this is presented in terms of the need to turn away from the kinds of conduct they used to indulge in (1.14; 4.2-4). Put positively, they are urged to be people who do what is 'good' (2.12, 15, 20; 3.6, 10-17; 4.19), who are holy just as God is holy (1.15-16). But this instruction to do good is clearly related to the specific situation of suffering in which they find themselves, where they are criticized and maligned by their non-Christian neighbours: 'Conduct yourselves well among the Gentiles, so that, though they slander you as evildoers, they may see your good deeds and glorify God on the day of visitation' (2.12). As this verse hints, it may not be until the end, and the final judgement, that the Christians are finally vindicated. Nonetheless, the author's hope is that if they do what is good, they may even now be able to silence hostile criticism: 'For this is the will of God, that by doing good you should put to silence the ignorance of foolish people' (2.15, ESV). What this implies is that what the author sees as 'good' conduct will be recognized as good by non-Christians as well as those within the Church. What, then, does the author specifically commend as good behaviour and how does this relate to the Church's difficult existence in the world?

The section of the letter from 2.11–3.12, the section including the so-called 'household code' material, is the most relevant place to find the author's instructions on good Christian conduct. The first specific instruction, which parallels Paul's earlier exhortation to the Roman Christians (Rom. 13.1-7), is to 'be subject to every human institution [or 'creature' – the translation of *ktisis* here is open to debate] for the Lord's sake, whether to the emperor as supreme, or to governors, who are sent by him to punish those who do evil and reward those who do good' (2.13-14). In other words, as the following verse implies (2.15), Christians are to behave, as far as possible, in a way that the emperor and his governors will recognize and reward as good, including being subject to their rule. This is summed up in the concise instruction of 2.17: 'honour everyone, love the family of believers [Gk: *adelphotēs*, 'brotherhood'], fear God, honour the emperor'. Although this instruction does, rather crucially, express a degree of resistance to imperial demands, as we shall see below, it clearly urges the Christian recipients of the letter to live in a way which positively respects Rome's rule, honouring the emperor, just as they honour all people (and not just believers, who are specifically to be loved).

What 'doing good' means is further specified in the various sections of the domestic or household code material, which, like other New Testament examples (see Col. 3.18–4.1; Eph. 5.21-6.9), addresses various groups within the household structure. Slaves, addressed first, are to submit to their masters, even those who are wicked, and even when they are unfairly beaten (2.18-20). Wives are likewise to submit to their husbands, whether or not those husbands are believers (3.1-6). Indeed, the decent and submissive conduct of such women is intended to function as a form of missionary appeal, with the aim of gaining their husbands for the faith. Again we see how the kind of good conduct urged upon the Christians is intended to be behaviour which outsiders will see and affirm as good and attractive, commending the believers as people of good character. Indeed, Balch sees the household code as used by 'the author of 1 Peter to stress the importance of Christians seeking peace and harmony in their household relationships and with society' (Balch 1981: 105).

By contrast, Elliott argues that 'the household code...was used to promote both the *internal solidarity* of the sectarian movement and its *external distinction* from Gentile motives and manners' (Elliott 1981: 231, my emphasis; cf. pp. 115, 140, 229). On the latter view, however, it is difficult to see why the code of conduct presented in the letter should bear such striking similarity to that which was widely promoted as socially respectable in Greco-Roman teaching on appropriate management of the household (see Balch 1981). Unlike the broadly comparable codes in Colossians and Ephesians, here in 1 Peter there is no address to slave owners, and only a brief instruction to husbands (3.7). The focus is on the 'weaker' parties in such household relationships, who were particularly likely to experience suffering if they were perceived to be deviating from socially and religiously acceptable ways.

Indeed, it is clear that what 1 Peter means by 'good' conduct is, to a considerable extent, behaviour which is socially respectable: honouring the emperor, submitting to masters and husbands, not provoking trouble or conflict. This may be precisely the kind of thing in view in the enigmatic word used in 4.15, that Christians should be careful not to bring suffering on themselves because of genuine wrong-doing on their part: 'Let none of you suffer as a murderer, or a thief, or an evildoer, nor as a meddler in other people's business'. This last phrase translates one highly unusual Greek word, probably coined by the author of 1 Peter: *allotriepiskopos*. As the translation given above implies, the word probably refers to someone who meddles in the affairs of other people. This should not be seen as a merely trivial matter, such as we might refer to as interfering, or sticking one's nose into other people's business. Rather, as Jeannine

Brown (2006) has recently shown, such 'meddling' was seen by some Greek and Roman writers as a rather serious sort of misbehaviour, which involved moving outside one's assigned sphere, transgressing social boundaries, and as such was seen as socially disruptive and politically dangerous.

So in these sections at least, 1 Peter seems to urge its readers to a broadly conformist and compliant attitude towards civic authority and social expectation. In Balch's terms, the author is seeking to assimilate Christian practice to broader social expectations, to defend the Christians against the charge that they reject and subvert social norms, and thereby to lessen criticism and hostility against them. As Warren Carter (2004) has recently suggested, this quiet (external) conformity represents an understandable strategy for survival in a situation where the readers have little power and little opportunity to resist the pressures to participate in the range of social and religious practices that constitute honouring the emperor. Nonetheless, Carter suggests, the letter does urge a kind of hidden, inner resistance, since the readers - while outwardly conforming to the expectations of the wider society and the Roman authorities - inwardly reverence Christ in their hearts (3.15), thus sustaining a sense of distance and resistance to the cultural hegemony that surrounds them. We might note similar instructions in the Pauline letters, not only in the call to obedience to the emperor in Rom. 13.1-7 (cf. 1 Tim. 2.1-3; Tit. 3.1-2) and the household code material (Col. 3.18-4.1; Eph. 5.21-6.9; 1 Tim. 6.1-2; Tit. 2.2-10), but also in the exhortation to 'live a quiet life' and live in a way acceptable to outsiders (1 Thess. 4.11-12; 2 Thess. 3.12).

But is Carter right to suggest that the author of 1 Peter expects and urges his readers, given the pressures of their context, to 'go all the way' in honouring the emperor, even to the extent of participating in the imperial cult - the widespread and diverse forms of cult in which the emperor was revered and worshipped (see esp. Price 1984; Mitchell 1993, I: 100-17)? Does the letter urge complete outward conformity to the world? Put differently, alongside its teaching that readers should 'do good', that is, should seek to gain the favour of outsiders by living in ways that are respectable and conformist, are there also ways in which 1 Peter urges its readers to resist the expectations of wider society, and specifically the demands of the empire?

Suffering as a Christian and Resisting the Empire

There are indeed various respects in which we might see the letter resisting the demands of the empire, and resisting pressures to conform. First, it is worth reconsidering the very opening of the letter, and the terms in which the author describes the addressees. They are God's chosen refugees of the Diaspora (1.1). As we have already seen (Chapter 3), these terms show the letter's dependence on Jewish tradition, specifically the LXX. But it is also significant to note how these terms evoke a particular narrative, which defines the identity of the addressees in specific ways. The readers are depicted, in terms drawn from the experience of the people of Israel, as those who have been scattered, made strangers and refugees.

A further piece of this picture is presented in 5.13, where, in the letter's closing remarks, the author sends greetings from 'your co-elect sister [church?] in Babylon'. As most commentators agree, this reference to Babylon is almost certainly a reference to Rome, which is thus identified as the centre of the imperial power, the power which has conquered Jerusalem and sent God's people into exile, scattering them as strangers in the world, just as Babylon did many centuries earlier. In other words, by using this set of terms - refugees, Diaspora, Babylon - the author invites his readers to understand themselves and their situation as analogous to the experience of Israel under Babylon's oppressive rule. Rome is identified as Babylon, and thus as the evil city, the imperial power, which oppresses God's people, bringing suffering and exile upon them.

This depiction of who they are in the world invites the readers of 1 Peter to understand themselves as people dislocated from the empire, not 'at home' in society, and thus stands in some contrast to the kind of perspective promoted in imperial ideology and cult. Augustus was hailed, in the province of Asia, in a famous inscription from 9 BCE, as the embodiment of good news, the saviour who had established peace and marked the beginning of all things; the calendar was thus rearranged to begin the new year on Augustus's birthday (see Price 1984: 54-55). The record of Augustus's deeds, the *Res Gestae*, inscribed in both Latin and Greek on the walls of the temple of Roma and Augustus in Ancyra, in central Asia Minor (see Map on p. ix), commemorates his establishment of peace through conquest, and his acclamation as *pater patriae* (father of the fatherland). So there is a sense in which, ideologically, the readers of 1 Peter are given a distinct perspective on who they are, in terms drawn from Israel's experience on the underside of empire, which dislocates them from the (imperial) world in which they live. Correspondingly, the positive description of their identity in 2.4-10, as we have already seen (Chapter 4), draws heavily on Israel's scriptures to proclaim the glorious status of this people of God, God's chosen race, who form a new family of brothers and sisters (2.17; 5.9) waiting for their inheritance in heaven (1.4).

But all this could be seen along the lines Carter suggests, as resources for the 'internal', hidden, resistance which the Christians of 1 Peter sustain, at the same time as they outwardly conform to the imperial demands for loyalty. What about any forms of practical, concrete resistance? Crucial here is 2.13-17, a text, we have already seen, that essentially appears to urge an obedience to imperial authority.

Nonetheless, in this very text, there are also significant indications of a certain critical distance being expressed. First, in 2.13, it is important to note that the appeal for submission to the emperor is framed as part of an appeal to submit to every human *ktisis* - meaning here 'that which has been created', which may refer to human 'institutions' (so NRSV, ESV) or to human 'creatures' (so Elliott 2000: 489). The emperor, in other words, is only one instance - and by no means a unique one - where this pattern of conduct is appropriate. Second, the author's description of the emperor as a *human* institution, or a human creature, seems calculated to oppose any notion that the emperor was divine - as was commonly proclaimed (for example, in the idea that the living emperor was *divi filius*, son of the divine, his predecessor having been divinized at death; or in the recorded acclamation of Domitian as 'our lord and god' [Suetonius, *Domitian* 13]). Third, the author insists that Christians are 'free people' (*eleutheroi*), or rather, are slaves (only) to God, even though he makes clear that this freedom does not provide a justification for acting in ways that are wicked (2.16). Fourth, and most important, there is the precise and careful wording of 2.17: 'Honour everyone, love the family of believers, fear God (*ton theon phobeisthe*), honour the emperor (*ton basilea timate*)'. The crucial distinction, of course, is between 'fear' and 'honour'. The verb *phobeomai*, to fear, here means 'to have profound reverence and respect for deity, with the implication of awe bordering on fear - "to reverence, to worship" ' (Louw-Nida's *Lexicon*). In other words, while the emperor is to be honoured, just as all people are, he is not to be worshipped; that belongs only to God.

Drawing this particular line is, as the later martyr-accounts show, sufficient to be regarded as obstinate resistance to the demands of the empire. For example, in the *Acts of the Scillitan Martyrs* (180 CE), exactly the same distinction is drawn. The proconsul, Saturninus, urges the Christians to swear by the genius of the emperor - that is, by his (divine) spirit, that which represents the self-identity of each male person. They reply: 'We have none other whom we worship (*timeamus*) but our Lord God who is in heaven... Honour (*honorem*) to Caesar as Caesar, but worship (*timorem*) only to God' (*Act. Scil.* 8-9). The early Christians often reiterated their willingness to be subject to the emperor, sometimes alluding to Romans 13, but at the same time refused to worship the emperor or the Roman gods; and this was regarded as an obstinate refusal to conform, a form of resistance that carried the death penalty (cf. *Martyrdom of Polycarp* 10–11). We have already noted a similar practice in Pliny's dealings with the Christians of Pontus-Bithynia in the early second century: to prove their innocence from the charge of being a Christian, a person had not only to curse Christ, but also to offer cult to the Roman gods and the emperor's image.

As we have already noted, the tendency in most recent scholarship on 1 Peter is to regard the suffering which the letter addresses as a consequence of informal public hostility rather than imperial persecution. Indeed, 2.13-17 is often seen as evidence to support this picture. Steven Bechtler, for example, puts it clearly:

> the one passage in the letter in which the emperor is explicitly mentioned - 2.13-17 - tells against imperial persecution. Here the letter enjoins fear of God and honor of the emperor in a single breath and commands subjection to the emperor as ὑπερέχων [supreme]. Nor does 1 Peter elsewhere exhibit the kind of hostility to, or at least wariness of, Rome to be expected in a document dealing with imperial persecution (Bechtler 1998: 50).

However, given the rather precise parallels in later accounts of Christian martyrdom, 2.13-17 actually fits well into a setting where a measured but conscious resistance to imperial demands is required. Indeed, it is precisely such a setting that explains the careful wording of 2.17.

The particular path the author treads between conformity and resistance may also be illustrated from 4.12-19, the text where the fiery ordeals suffered by the readers are most vividly and explicitly discussed. The suffering is depicted as a sharing in the sufferings of Christ, suffering in his name, and thus a cause for rejoicing and blessing (vv. 13-14). The contrast is then drawn between suffering as a murderer, thief, evildoer, or 'meddler', and suffering 'as a Christian' (vv. 15-16). In keeping with his appeal to the readers to 'do good' the author insists that they should be sure never to be guilty of such crimes and misdemeanours as are listed first; this would indeed be a cause for shame. But the accusation of being a Christian is another matter. This label should be borne with pride, not shame, and regarded as a means to glorify God (4.16).

The appearance of the word 'Christian' (*Christianos*) here is interesting. It appears only three times in the New Testament (Acts 11.26; 26.28; 1 Pet. 4.16), and appears not to have been known to Paul, at least so far as the evidence of his letters allows us to conclude. It becomes an established Christian self-designation only rather later, beginning with Ignatius in the early second century and becoming prominent nearer the end of the second century. In Acts 11.26, Luke reports that 'it was in Antioch that the disciples were first called "Christians" ' (NRSV). However, Luke does not specifically say that it was at this time - in the very early years of the Christian mission - that the label arose, and there are good reasons to think that it originated somewhat later, perhaps around the late 50s or early 60s in the first century CE. The form of the word, with its *-ianos* ending, indicates that it is a Latinism, that is, a word formed in Latin, or in a Latin way, and then transliterated into Greek. Most scholars have concluded that the term originated not with the Christians themselves but with outsiders, who labelled the members of this new movement as members of Christ's circle, supporters of Christ. There are various theories as to the place and context of the label's origin - among the populus or administration of Rome, at the appearance of Paul before Festus (Acts 26; Botermann 1996), or among Roman officials when they encountered Christians in Antioch and elsewhere. Certainly, given the Latin form of the name, and other aspects of the wording of Luke's report in Acts 11.26, there is a good deal to be said for

the view that it originated in the encounter between
Christians and Roman officials (see Peterson 1946).

Not only was the name an outsiders' label for members of
this new movement, but it also quickly became the crucial
focus in trials of the Christians. During Nero's persecution of
the Christians in the mid-60s, other supposed crimes may
have been an initial basis for the arrest of suspects. But soon
the name itself became a sufficient indicator of criminality,
and by the time of Pliny's trials it is the name itself, rather
than any demonstrable 'associated crimes', that is the basis for
condemnation. Thus emerged a focus on the *nomen ipsum*,
the name itself, as the crucial issue: 'Are you a Christian?'
became the key question for a prosecutor, just as 'I am a
Christian' became the fatal declaration of the martyr.

This background is important for understanding 1 Pet. 4.12-
19 and for seeing the interesting part this text plays in the
making of 'Christian' identity. In keeping with his insistence
that Christians should be people who 'do good', the author is
insistent that they should never be guilty of the kinds of
crimes of which others may accuse them. (Indeed, we know
that stock accusations of murder, cannibalism, incest, and so
on, were frequently levelled at the early Christians.) However,
the author is well aware that the label 'Christian' may also be
used as a form of accusation, a negative label, that functions
to condemn and thus is a cause of suffering. In this case, the
author insists, the label is to be accepted with pride, and
boldly acknowledged. Suffering 'as a Christian' is no cause for
shame, but rather a means to glorify God. In this text,
therefore, 1 Peter not only gives us a unique, early window
into the kinds of context in which the label 'Christian' might
be used, but also represents the first Christian attempt to
claim the label as a positive one, to be borne with pride,
despite the fact that outsiders regard it as a cause of
condemnation and shame. Thus, 1 Peter marks a first step
in the process by which the label 'Christian' eventually
became the one that insiders would use to designate
themselves. A little later, Ignatius expresses the desire 'not

only to be *called* a Christian but to *be* one' (*Letter to the Magnesians* 4.1; cf. *Letter to the Romans* 3.2), a further indication of the process by which the name became not just a label outsiders would use but a 'true' designation of what the believer is.

From a social-psychological perspective, this may be regarded as a strategy of social creativity, an attempt to alter the negative implications of specific designations of group members (see Horrell 2007a). Other groups too, who find themselves stigmatized and negatively labelled, have responded by claiming those labels – with a kind of polemical pride – as positive self-descriptions, challenging and attempting to reverse the verdict of society upon them. The classic example, social psychologists note, is the attempt to overturn the negative associations of being black through the slogan 'black is beautiful'. We might also think of the ways in which the derogatory label 'queer' has been used by gay people themselves, as a provocative and positive self-naming.

More generally, in terms of our question about resistance to the empire, it is clear that in the name Christian the conflict between church and empire finds a focal point, and in 1 Peter a line of resistance is drawn. Unlike the normal form of criminal trial, where the pressure is exerted to make the suspects confess their crime, the pressure on the Christians is to disown the name, and to prove their religio-political loyalty by worshipping the gods, praying to the emperor or swearing by his genius. (Precisely this rather topsy-turvy kind of trial, where the pressure is to deny the crime, rather than confess it, is the focus of Tertullian's ridicule, in his *Apology* 2–3.) At this particular point of conflict, the author of 1 Peter insists, the name is to be boldly and proudly borne, whatever pressure and suffering may result. In such situations, Christians are to entrust themselves to God, a faithful creator, whose judgement on the world is about to begin (4.17-19).

Conforming and Resisting: Making Sense of 1 Peter

How, then, are we to make sense of 1 Peter's stance towards the world and the empire? How can we reconcile the prominent theme of 'doing good' and honouring the emperor with the clear stance of distance and resistance? As the Balch–Elliott debate shows, along with a good deal of other work on the letter, scholarship has tended to emphasize one aspect or the other – either the tendency to assimilate and accommodate to the world, or the desire to strengthen the distinctive life and character of the Church. Indeed, as we shall see in the final chapter, differing assessments of 1 Peter, in this and other respects, account in part for the diverse reactions of contemporary readers to the letter.

What we need, in my view, are perspectives that can enable us to move beyond a somewhat unsatisfactory categorization of a text as either conformist or resistant. Too often, scholars have depicted certain New Testament texts as radical and resistant to the empire, and others as conservative and conformist, or have argued about whether a text like 1 Peter is one thing or the other. One notable and interesting attempt to move beyond the alternatives of the Balch–Elliott debate is presented by Miroslav Volf (1994), who argues that 1 Peter – and specifically its household code – offers 'an example of differentiated acceptance and rejection of the surrounding culture' (p. 22). According to Volf, '[t]hough 1 Peter does not envisage changing social structures, Christians nevertheless have a mission in the world' (p. 24) and are seen by the author of the letter as having a missionary responsibility to live out their 'distance' from society, in a way which exhibits what Volf calls 'soft difference'. Volf thus finds in 1 Peter a valuable model for the contemporary church, situated as it is 'in modern, rapidly changing, pluralistic societies' (p. 27). One thing missing from Volf's essay, though, is attention to the specifically *imperial* context which 1 Peter addresses and hence to the particular kinds of strategies by which vulnerable social groups might negotiate their existence under the ruling powers.

An alternative approach, which offers the basis for a more nuanced perspective, with a particular focus on the ways in which the socially weak exercise forms of resistance to the powerful, may build on the work of the political scientist James Scott, particularly in his influential book *Domination and the Arts of Resistance* (1990). Scott stresses that open revolt and outright resistance are the unusual, and often short-lived, forms of resistance to domination. Scott's interest is in the manifold 'everyday' ways by which the subordinate express resistance, while in other respects remaining within the bounds of expected conformity. These strategies of resistance may include the 'hidden transcripts' in which the oppressed, when out of sight of their masters, tell different stories about the world and their place in it. 1 Peter's description of the readers' identity as the chosen people of God, scattered and made homeless by the actions of Babylon, might be seen as just such an 'alternative' vision, shared among the early Christian communities. Other modes of resistance include humour and parody, evasion and poaching, and all kinds of practical and linguistic means to sustain some critical distance from complete and willing obedience. Again, we have seen how 1 Peter certainly draws a clear line of resistance, alongside a generally obedient and conformist stance: the emperor is not to be worshipped, only God; and the name Christian is not to be denied, whatever the pressures to abandon it. Orders to renounce the name and to worship the Roman gods are to be resisted.

Postcolonial studies also offer fruitful resources with which to illuminate the way in which 1 Peter seeks to negotiate the difficult task of living a Christian life in the empire. Postcolonialism, a field of growing influence in literary and cultural studies, and in biblical studies too, is concerned with the impact of colonialism/imperialism on societies and cultures, and is concerned in particular with the ways in which the colonized respond to the encounter with the colonial/imperial power, often through the literature produced in such settings. Although postcolonialism as a discipline is concerned with the impact of European colonialism from the sixteenth century onwards, its perspectives and concepts can be fruitfully applied to the Roman empire too. As in Scott's work, so too in the work of many postcolonial writers, notably Homi Bhabha, there is a stress on the ambivalent and complex relationship between colonizer and colonized, and between conformity and resistance. Again, this can help us to avoid a too simple distinction between seeing texts like 1 Peter as *either* resistant to empire *or* conformist. As Stephen Moore puts it: 'For Bhabha, resistance and complicity coexist in different measures in each and every colonial subject' (2006: 110). Indeed, another of Bhabha's stresses is on what he calls hybridity, which is to say that the cultural identities of both colonizer and colonized are formed and articulated in the 'space' of their encounter and interaction, rendering the identity of each, in a sense, hybrid, mixed. A good example of this in 1 Peter would be the name 'Christian'. As we have seen, its very form reflects the colonizer's language (Latin), and it originates as a hostile outsiders' label; but it gets claimed by the insiders, the members of the Christian movement in Asia Minor and elsewhere, as a designation of who they are.

Scott and Bhabha also help us to see how a writer like the author of 1 Peter is not being simply conformist, or accommodating the church to the world, even if he does take a less radical, anti-Roman stance than, say, the author of Revelation. The resistance expressed by the author of 1 Peter is different, more subtle and muted, but it is resistance nonetheless. I have elsewhere suggested the label 'polite resistance' to epitomize the stance of 1 Peter to the empire (Horrell 2007b). And, as we have seen in discussing 2.17 above, this kind of stance – willing to be good and obedient citizens as far as possible, but drawing a clear line of resistance at certain points – was influential in the ongoing story of Christianity's tense relationship with Rome and established a pattern many others would follow.

So, then, 1 Peter makes an important contribution to the making of Christian identity and the negotiation of the Church's existence in the Roman empire. It does so specifically in relation to the name 'Christian', which would eventually become the standard designation for members of this young religious movement; 1 Peter makes the first attempt to claim the name as a positive badge to be proudly worn. It does so more generally in the way it positions the Church in the world, and specifically vis-à-vis the empire. 1 Peter does not depict the empire as the embodiment of evil, nor the emperor as the Beast, unlike the book of Revelation. The author of 1 Peter is much more concerned to ensure a peaceful existence in the world, so far as that is possible; and he urges Christians to be people who do good and avoid trouble. Nonetheless, he is also clear about the respect in which Christians must resist the empire's demands, even if suffering be the result.

Further Reading

The monographs of Balch (1981) and Elliott (1981), and Elliott's (2000) commentary, are listed at the end of Chapter 1. The two essays in which they engage directly in debate are:

Balch, David L., 'Hellenization/Acculturation in 1 Peter', in Charles H. Talbert (ed.), *Perspectives on First Peter* (Macon, GA: Mercer University Press, 1986), 79-101.

Elliott, John H., '1 Peter, Its Situation and Strategy: A Discussion with David Balch', in Charles H. Talbert (ed.), *Perspectives on First Peter* (Macon, GA: Mercer University Press, 1986), 61-78.

For critical discussion, see the works of Bechtler and others listed in Chapter 3. Two alternative perspectives, attempting in different ways to understand the way 1 Peter positions the Church in relation to its wider society, are:

> Miller, Larry, 'La protestation sociale dans la première lettre de Pierre', *Social Compass* 46 (1999), 521-43.

> Volf, Miroslav, 'Soft Difference: Reflections on the Relation between Church and Culture in 1 Peter', *Ex Auditu* 10 (1994), 15-30.

On the imperial cult, and the wider socio-political context in Asia Minor at the time of 1 Peter, see the two volumes by Mitchell, listed in Chapter 3, and:

> Price, Simon R.F., *Rituals and Power: The Roman Imperial Cult in Asia Minor* (Cambridge: Cambridge University Press, 1984).

On the ways in which early Christian communities in Asia Minor sought to fit into this imperial society, see:

> Harland, Philip A., *Associations, Synagogues, and Congregations* (Minneapolis, MN: Fortress, 2003).

Important arguments concerning the origins and significance of the name 'Christian' are presented in the following works. For a social-psychological perspective on the significance of the label 'Christian', see my essay (Horrell 2007a) listed in Chapter 3:

> Botermann, Helga, *Das Judenedikt des Kaisers Claudius: Römischer Staat und Christiani im 1 Jahrhundert* (Stuttgart: Franz Steiner, 1996).

> Peterson, Erik, 'Christianus', in idem, *Frühkirche, Judentum und Gnosis* (Rome, Freiburg, Vienna: Herder, 1959 [1946]), 64-87.

On the term *allotriepiskopos* ('one who meddles in others' affairs', 1 Pet. 4.15), see:

> Brown, Jeannine K., 'Just a Busybody? A Look at the Greco-

Roman Topos of Meddling for Defining *allotriepiskopos* in 1 Peter 4.15', *Journal of Biblical Literature* 125 (2006), 549-68.

Scott's work on forms of 'everyday' resistance is found in:

> Scott, James C., *Domination and the Arts of Resistance: Hidden Transcripts* (New Haven and London: Yale University Press, 1990).

For applications of this perspective to the Gospels and Paul's letters see:

> Horsley, Richard A. (ed.), *Hidden Transcripts and the Arts of Resistance: Applying the Work of James C. Scott to Jesus and Paul* (Semeia Studies, 48; Atlanta, GA: SBL, 2004).

And specifically to 1 Peter, see:

> Carter, Warren, 'Going All the Way? Honoring the Emperor and Sacrificing Wives and Slaves in 1 Peter 2.13–3.6', in Amy-Jill Levine and Maria Mayo Robbins (eds), *A Feminist Companion to the Catholic Epistles* (London and New York: T&T Clark, 2004), 14-33.

For applications of postcolonial perspectives to biblical studies, see:

> Moore, Stephen D., *Empire and Apocalypse: Postcolonialism and the New Testament* (Sheffield: Sheffield Phoenix Press, 2006).

> Sugirtharajah, R.S. (ed.), *The Postcolonial Biblical Reader* (Oxford: Blackwell, 2006).

And specifically to 1 Peter, see:

> Horrell, David G., 'Between Conformity and Resistance: Beyond the Balch-Elliott Debate Towards a Postcolonial Reading of 1 Peter', in Robert L. Webb and Betsy Bauman-Martin (eds), *Reading 1 Peter with New Eyes: Methodological Reassessments of the Letter of First Peter* (LNTS; London and New York: T&T Clark, 2007) [=2007b].

6

ASSESSING 1 PETER: AN AMBIVALENT LEGACY?

We have studied various aspects of 1 Peter, from its genre and structure, its content and traditions, through to its use of Jewish scripture and its stance towards the Roman empire. Each of these areas, in its different way, has raised certain issues for contemporary readers. The question of how contemporary readers respond to the letter, and how we address the issues it raises, is the topic for this concluding chapter.

The first letter of Peter, despite its somewhat marginal status among the writings of the New Testament, has often received high praise. Martin Luther, for example, described this letter as 'one of the grandest of the New Testament, and it is the true, pure gospel' (Luther 1523: 10). More recently, Howard Marshall suggests that 'if one were to be shipwrecked on a desert island and allowed to have only one of the New Testament letters as a companion, then 1 Peter would be the ideal choice, so rich is its teaching, so warm its spirit, and so comforting its message in a hostile environment' (Marshall 1991: 12). It is not difficult to see why the letter should engender such reactions. Indeed, despite the fact that the letter does not receive as much scholarly attention as some other NT texts, there are plenty of reasons why 1 Peter is a theologically significant text that deserves more attention than it gets.

First, it is, as we have seen, a richly synthetic letter that draws together a range of Christian and biblical traditions (see Chapter 2). It is especially saturated in the Jewish scriptures. Moreover, unlike some of Paul's most influential letters (esp.

Galatians), and unlike 2 Peter, 1 Peter is a non-polemical writing: it does not direct itself against Christian opponents or 'false' teaching but rather presents its own positive message for its hard-pressed readers. Although it is, as we have seen, written to address a particular situation, it is not enmeshed in a particular dispute or argument in the same way that a good many of the other NT letters are. In short, because it is synthetic, non-polemical and compact 1 Peter presents a fine example of early Christian doctrinal and ethical instruction – *multum in parvo*, to quote a Latin phrase; or in more everyday terms, it packs a lot in.

Second, the letter is indeed full of *theology*. Howard Marshall suggests that '[t]he density of the theology of 1 Peter is quite remarkable' (2004: 657), while Ralph Martin goes so far as to say that '[p]robably no document in the New Testament is so theologically orientated as 1 Peter, if the description is taken in the strict sense of teaching about God' (1994: 104). Marshall distinguishes three categories of Christian belief, all of which are prominent in 1 Peter: doxological (that is, worship and praise of God), antagonistic (that is, opposition to evil) and soteriological (that is, orientated towards salvation which will be consummated in the future). As Marshall puts it: 'The Christian life is expressed in praise, worship and thanksgiving to God; it is lived in opposition to Satan and evil; and it derives its strength from the salvation bestowed by God in Christ and through the Holy Spirit' (2004: 648). Partly because 1 Peter is such a synthetic letter, filled with scriptural and early Christian tradition, its theology is dense and rich. For example, its opening thanksgiving is theologically and poetically impressive: 'Blessed be the God and Father of our Lord Jesus Christ, who by his great mercy has given you to be born anew into a living hope through the resurrection of Jesus Christ from the dead. . .' (1.3).

Third, any comment on the synthetic and traditional character of 1 Peter must be balanced by other important features of the letter, namely those respects in which the author uniquely or distinctively presents his interpretation of Christian doctrine. In some cases, 1 Peter is unique in the fullness with which it presents ideas which are only glimpsed elsewhere in the NT: for example, important to 1 Peter's Christology is the idea of Christ as the suffering one, who sets out a path for his followers to tread. In setting out this depiction of Jesus' suffering 1 Peter draws on the language and imagery of Isaiah 53 more fully and explicitly than any other NT text, helping to establish this prophetic text as an influential vehicle for conveying the significance of Christ's passion. Also distinctive, though much more enigmatic, are the descriptions of Christ's proclamation to the imprisoned spirits (3.18-22) and the indication that the gospel was preached to the dead (4.6).

Fourth, 1 Peter offers a particularly rich example of the ways in which the traditions of the Jewish scriptures and of early Christianity, particularly in Christology, were used to construct and sustain the identity of the Christian converts. 1 Peter contains some of the most memorable and splendid declarations of the glorious identity of the people of God found in the New Testament: 'you are a chosen people, a royal priesthood, a holy nation', and so on – phrases rendered even more memorable in their setting to music, for example, in John Ireland's anthem 'Greater Love Hath No Man'. Thus 1 Peter has played a very significant role in contributing to a developing sense of Christian identity, and filling that identity with terms, images and ideas which have become important to the Christian tradition.

Fifth, and finally, 1 Peter has been characterized as an epistle of hope. Its message for its readers centres around their sure hope of salvation, and the way this can serve to sustain and encourage them despite suffering and persecution. Thus the letter's teaching has an eschatological character, a sense of future hope which already pervades the present and transforms it, again a central theme in Christian theology. The letter also tries to help its readers to negotiate their difficult existence in a hostile world, cultivating a

balance between quietly conforming to wider social expectations, and at the same time sustaining a sense of distance
from the world, even resistance to it, living as strangers and
aliens. This attempt to set out a pattern for Christian living in
a hostile world has been both relevant and important to
Christians in many times and places, for whom the experience of social marginalization and public or official hostility
has been a real and pressing experience.

All this and more gives some indication of the theological
value of 1 Peter, its significant contribution to the making of
the Christian tradition. Yet, as we have already seen, these
influential and important aspects of the letter also raise
certain critical questions for contemporary interpreters.

The Church and Israel

As we saw in detail in Chapter 4, the author of 1 Peter draws
on the scriptures of Israel to describe the identity of this new
people of God, the Church. This is by no means a unique
move on the part of the author; on the contrary, most of the
New Testament writers do this in some way or other. But 1
Peter does represent a particularly rich and vivid example of
this in 2.9-10, where, as we have noted, a whole series of
Jewish scriptural labels is applied to the Church, including
the only NT application to Christians of the term *genos* (race,
family, or tribe). As such, 1 Peter raises a pressing question for
Christian theologians: Can the identity of the Church be
claimed and sustained without at the same time implying that
the Jews have lost their status as God's people?

What should we take as the implication of 1 Peter's use of
the Jewish scriptures in this way, and of the letter's silence
concerning the existence of non-Christian Jews? Marshall
notes that 'the question of the status of Jews who had not
become part of the Christian church is not discussed' in 1
Peter, and sees this as an indication of the fact that '[t]he
place of the church as the successor of Israel in the Old
Testament is taken for granted' in this letter (2004: 650). Does

1 Peter thus imply that the Church has replaced Israel as the people of God - a position generally known as supersessionism (cf. Mt. 21.43; Gal. 4.21-31)? Or does its silence about the status and existence of the ethnic, 'historic' Israel suggest, or at least allow, the view that the Church's adoption of Jewish titles and identity does not deprive the Jews of that identity, and their salvation is secure on the basis of their original covenant promises (cf. Rom. 11.26, 29)? Or might it assume the view that the Church (of both Jews and Gentiles) constitutes an 'elect' remnant into which 'all Israel' will ultimately be reincorporated in some kind of eschatological resolution (cf. Rom. 9-11, esp. 11.25-32)?

Achtemeier is insistent that what we find in 1 Peter 'is evidently not an instance of anti-Semitism... The reason is simply that for the author of 1 Peter, Israel has become the controlling metaphor for the new people of God, and as such its rhetoric has passed without remainder into that of the Christian community' (Achtemeier 1996: 72). The lack of any anti-Jewish polemic (contrast, e.g., Jn 8.22-44; 1 Thess. 2.14-16) or any explicit statement about the superiority of Christianity's 'new' covenant to Judaism's 'old' one (contrast, e.g., Heb. 7.18-19; 8.6-13; 9.11-15; *Letter of Barnabas* 16.5-8) might indeed seem to relieve 1 Peter of the charge of being anti-Jewish or anti-Semitic. On the other hand, if it is true, as Achtemeier puts it, that 'the language and hence the reality of Israel pass *without remainder* into the language and hence the reality of the new people of God' (1996: 69) then that would seem to imply that Israel's continued existence is implicitly denied, and that the Church has indeed replaced Israel. Should we then read 1 Peter's silence about historic Israel as a 'deafening silence', as Betsy Bauman-Martin (2007) has suggested, that reflects its strategy of 'ideological imperialism', a form of colonialism that robs Israel of its special identity and usurps it for the benefit of the Church?

These are difficult questions, not only for the historical understanding of 1 Peter - what did the author and addressees think, and mean to imply, about the Jewish

community and its continued existence? – but also because
they impinge upon contemporary discussions of the relations
between Jews and Christians. There has been considerable
recent study exploring the possibly anti-Jewish content and
impact of NT and other early Christian texts, often conducted, whether explicitly or implicitly, with an awareness of
the contemporary agenda, and especially the need for a
careful reassessment of Christian views of Judaism in a post-
Holocaust world. In terms of 1 Peter's particular contribution
– for good or bad – to this subject the key question seems to
me the silence of the letter concerning the status and fate of
'unbelieving' Israel, the Jews. It is beyond dispute that the
letter, like many other early Christian documents, applies to
the Church Jewish labels and identity-markers, thus appro-
priating Israel's scriptures as its own. The question is whether
its silence can be taken to allow theological room for a
positive answer to the question about Israel's continued
existence – in other words, as George Lindbeck puts it, that
the Church can and should be seen as 'Israel' but in
conjunction with the conviction that the Jews *also* remain
'Israel', that 'the covenant with the Jews has never been
revoked' (Lindbeck 2000: 358). Alternatively, the silence
might be taken to imply a more (for us) problematic claim,
that the Church has taken over and replaced Israel as the
people of God. If that is so, then – as with other NT
documents like the Gospel of John – contemporary interpreters have to face the fact that this text may leave us with
something of a difficult, ambivalent heritage.

A more positive reading of the silence of 1 Peter on the
status of historic Israel may or may not reflect what the author
meant to imply by his silence, nor necessarily an answer he
would accept, but the alternative – a clear supersessionism –
seems to me a problematic contemporary stance, for all sorts
of moral and theological reasons. (Jews are then regarded as
having lost their status as God's people, through their failure
to believe in Christ. Theologically this raises the problem Paul
saw so clearly: What has become of God's faithfulness to the

covenant? Morally, this stance not only makes respectful dialogue difficult, but also is in danger of legitimating the kind of anti-Semitism that has already borne terrible consequences in Europe and elsewhere.) Whatever the intentions of the author of 1 Peter – something to which we can have no access, except insofar as we have his text to read – the silence of the text about the status of Israel makes it possible to appropriate the text within a wider theology which constructs a positive place both for the Church and for Israel, more so than with texts that explicitly make negative statements about Israel's rejection.

Social Conformity and Feminist Critique

We have also seen how the author of 1 Peter urges his readers to 'do good', by which he means to conduct themselves in ways that broadly conform to wider social expectations. They are to be good citizens, honouring the emperor and being appropriately subject to all. For slaves and wives this means submitting to their masters and husbands, suffering quietly under wicked masters (2.18-20) and attempting to win unbelieving husbands for the faith (3.1-6). In this way, the author hopes that Christians will be able to negate criticism of their way of life. As we have seen, this does not mean that he wants them to conform entirely to the expectations and customs of the world in which they live. On the contrary, there is also a clear call for resistance, and for loyalty to one's identity as a Christian, even when suffering results. Nonetheless, this is a 'polite resistance', flavoured with a desire to conform and obey as far as possible, including in ways which may involve suffering, not least for slaves and women.

How readers respond to this teaching depends in considerable part on their own ethical and political convictions, though these are not often made explicit. Ralph Martin, for example, suggests that in 1 Peter:

[t]here is no call to disobedience, whether civil or activist.
The ethical admonitions operate within the limit of 'what is
possible': honour to those in power, both good and evil-
minded (2.17; 3.17) and a caution to stay within the
contemporary social structures as submissive and peace-
making... The 'interim ethic' that lives in the present in
hope of a divine vindication in the coming age is very much
what 1 Peter's eschatological encouragement to 'endure
until the end' is all about (Martin 1994: 130).

Martin clearly sees 1 Peter's message as particularly relevant
to 'several parts of the world to which the Christian gospel is
introduced as a provocation to resistance, a disturbance
within the social order...' (p. 90). What Martin appears to
have in view here is the kind of stance represented by
liberation theology, where the gospel is understood to
demand a preferential and revolutionary option for the
poor, and their release from poverty and oppression through
radical social change. Martin seems to imply that 1 Peter
(rightly) opposes such a gospel, and calls Christians instead to
remain obediently within the social structures of their day.

Given such a reading of 1 Peter and its contemporary value,
it is no surprise to find that those whose contemporary
commitments are different take a very different view of the
letter. A liberation theologian might perhaps agree with
Martin about the force of 1 Peter's teaching, but conclude
that 1 Peter ought therefore to be resisted and regarded as
problematic. Feminist scholars in particular, with their focus
on liberation and equality for women, have often been critical
of 1 Peter, because of the way in which it urges wives to
submit to their husbands, to attempt to 'win them over' by
pure and quiet conduct. Kathleen Corley presents a particularly forceful critique of 1 Peter in this regard. Corley sees 1
Peter's call to slaves and wives to imitate the suffering Christ
by quietly and submissively accepting their suffering as a
disastrous stance that 'merely perpetuates a cycle of
victimization, violence, and abuse in domestic situations'.
She continues:

> The glorification of suffering, like that found in 1 Peter, is seen to glorify all suffering and in fact holds up the victim as a model for women... Thus, the myth of Jesus as 'Suffering Servant' should not be made into a model for Christian life, particularly for Christian women... Of all Christian Testament texts, the message of 1 Peter is the most harmful in the context of women's lives. Its particular message of the suffering Christ as a model for Christian living leads to precisely the kinds of abuses that feminists fear... The basic message of 1 Peter does not reflect God's liberating Word (Corley 1995: 354-57).

Corley's striking claim, then, is that far from being one of the best books in the New Testament, 1 Peter is perhaps the worst, and does not reflect the liberating word of the gospel.

It is interesting to note that, broadly speaking, Martin and Corley agree in their reading of what 1 Peter says: the letter does teach that Christians should obediently remain within the social structures of their day. Where they disagree is over the question as to whether that stance should be affirmed as the appropriate pattern of conduct for contemporary Christians or whether it should be exposed as a dangerous and damaging ethic that does not belong as part of a liberating gospel. Other interpreters, by contrast, offer somewhat different readings of 1 Peter, arguing that it does not merely keep suffering women and slaves in their place, nor urge social conformity and submission, but rather upholds their dignity and equality and constructs the Christian community as a distinctive and cohesive community. Paul Achtemeier, for example, interprets 3.1-7 against the backdrop of other early Christian texts on women and marriage:

> That the Christian faith inherently meant equal status for women in the sight of God is evident from such a passage as Gal 3:28, and from the important role played by women in the early church... [T]his passage [i.e. 3.1-7] intends to say nothing about the subordination of women to men in general, nor even within Christian marriage, but intends to be understood primarily within the context of a Christian

wife married to an unbelieving husband (Achtemeier 1996: 207-208).

Achtemeier continues, focusing on what he sees conveyed by verse 7:

> Although nothing is said in vv. 1-6 about the general status of women within the Christian community, or within Christian marriage, that status can be deduced from v. 7, addressed to Christian husbands...the author's intention [is] to point up the differences between women in a non-Christian and in a Christian situation, and the equality they enjoy in the latter... The glimpse this gives of the status of a Christian woman within the Christian family, as well as in the Christian community, shows that the emancipation of women is far from diminished, and that their equality is in fact enjoined as a Christian duty...upon Christian men (Achtemeier 1996: 208-209).

In short, Achtemeier argues that 1 Peter's advice to wives is geared to the specific situation of relations with a non-Christian husband, and that the author's instruction to husbands shows that his view of *Christian* marriage is one of equality between the partners.

One may well find Achtemeier's portrait of 1 Peter as supporting emancipation and equality for women in Christian marriage appealing, more appealing than the portrait of the text as one that has appeared to sanction domestic abuse and taught women that their duty is to quietly endure such evil. However, that does not necessarily make it convincing as a reading of the text. It is telling that Achtemeier must appeal to other texts (e.g. Gal. 3.28) to find the idea of women's equality in early Christianity; even there it is arguable how far equality is in view, and it is certainly doubtful that 1 Pet. 3.7 offers any clear reiteration of such a conviction. Women are, after all, famously described here as 'the weaker sex'.

On the other hand, one may question how far it is justified to find the text culpable, as Corley does, for perpetuating the cycle of domestic abuse, and for cultivating a victim-ethic which encourages women to bear such suffering quietly rather than seek to resist or escape it. How are we to assess and resolve such different interpretations, and in what ways should we be critical of 1 Peter? To what extent can an appreciation of the historical context in which the text was produced help to guide and inform our reading of it? The next section addresses such questions.

Historical Criticism and Theological Interpretation

Historical study can perhaps help to some extent, by situating the text within the context of its original production. In this context, as we have seen, Christians were a small minority, suffering hostility and persecution from the wider public and the Roman administration (see Chapter 3). Given the challenges of such a situation, it is understandable that the author both seeks to encourage the readers by outlining their glorious new identity and sure hope of salvation and also urges them to endure suffering as Christ did, while seeking to live 'good' lives that will minimize the level of hostility they have to endure. In other words, the strategy of quiet conformity, within limits, makes some sense *as a survival strategy* in the situation where a powerless minority is oppressed due to both public and imperial hostility.

That historical, contextual situating of 1 Peter does not, of course, render it immune from criticism. Even at the time, and facing similar pressures, other early Christians called for a much more radical and outright separation from the wider society and resistance to imperial demands. The writer of the book of Revelation, for example, if he were to have read 1 Peter (there is no evidence that he actually did), might well have thought that the author had gone much too far in compromising with the world and with the Beast, that is, the emperor (cf. Rev. 13; 17-18). Nonetheless, viewing 1 Peter in the light of its context of production can help us to appreciate something of the dynamics that led the author to write as he did.

But with the letter's preservation as a document of apostolic instruction, and its eventual inclusion into the New Testament canon, it became a text with an authoritative status that would influence the shape of Christian doctrine and ethics across time and space, in contexts very different from those in which it arose. This history of effects is varied and complex, yet no doubt includes the use of 1 Peter - along with other similar NT texts - to justify and sustain the abuse of women, or the institution of slavery, or indeed to foster anti-Jewish or anti-Semitic attitudes and actions.

To regard some of these negative aspects of 1 Peter's legacy as part of the text's history of interpretation is not to deny that the text itself can sustain such meanings. Every text is susceptible to a range of interpretations, and meaning is made in the encounter between readers and texts; it does not somehow inhere in an objectively determinable authorial intention. 1 Peter *can* be read in ways which legitimate the suffering of slaves and women, or suggest that Israel has been replaced by the Church.

Both historical criticism and the study of the history of interpretation can perhaps have some role in helping to relativize such readings. Historical criticism, as we have seen, helps us to understand how and why the author wrote as he did, addressing a particular situation and perceiving particular needs on the part of his audience. The history of interpretation can help us to see how different readers have read and used the text differently over time, and in ways that are shaped by their own location, presuppositions and interests. It is not too hard, for example, to see a rather unholy alliance between political interests and biblical exegesis in uses of the Bible to justify slavery or racial segregation (see Meeks 1996; Burridge 2007).

A key question is how - if it is possible - to guard against such uses of the Bible. Careful exegesis is not enough; as Wayne Meeks shows, the pro-slavery interpreters can be seen to have had the better exegetical arguments on their side, even though we find their moral stance repugnant. Meeks and

Richard Burridge, in different ways, suggest that one way is to ensure that biblical interpretation takes place in an inclusive and diverse community, in which the voices of those oppressed by particular readings are included and heard. For those who read 1 Peter in an ecclesial context, it is also important to seek a theologically-informed and theologically-discerning approach to reading and using the Bible. Elucidating Christian doctrine and ethics is not simply a matter of lining up relevant biblical texts to see what they say, despite the tendency of some to see it this way. As Karl Barth famously summarized the task of theology, it 'does not ask what the apostles and prophets said but what we must say on the basis of the apostles and prophets' (1975: 16). That concise definition implies a careful attention to what 'the apostles and prophets' said, that is, to the witness of the Bible, but also insists that the contemporary task involves a discernment of what 'we' then must say, which is not simply a repetition of the words said long ago. And, in a somewhat circular way - or, put better, a way which involves constant but critical dialogue with the tradition - theology and Christian ethics are informed by the scriptures but also at the same time shape and inform a critical reading of those scriptures. Luther, for example, as is well known, found in the scriptures, specifically in Paul, a doctrine which he came to see as central to the Christian gospel: justification by faith. That doctrine then became a key for reading and interpreting the Bible - and for criticizing texts, like the epistle of James, which seemed, in Luther's view, to lack this important focus. In a broadly comparable way, liberation theologians find the theme of liberation in the Bible, in stories such as the Exodus and in the mission of Jesus (e.g. Lk. 4.16-21), and make this a key for their critical reading of scripture. It is worth noting, on this point, that the value of texts, and their ability to challenge and discomfort us, changes with time and context: while Luther saw James as of somewhat doubtful value, liberation theologians have found it a particularly valuable text, with its sharp criticism of the rich who oppress the poor and its call for righteous action. So the diverse texts of the Christian canon, 1 Peter included, remain a resource which, while needing critical engagement, can always challenge and unsettle established and comfortable consensuses. But 1 Peter, and other biblical texts, are not only read within the context of the Church's life, but also in the context of the academy or university, where a wide range of voices, secular and religious, are engaged in conversation about the text. This, I want to suggest, is all to the good. A range of perspectives – some sympathetic to the text, some hostile to it – can help to challenge and to sharpen our understanding of it and its impact. Some Christians, for example, may be deeply uncomfortable with the reading of 1 Peter offered by Corley, which implicates the text in the history of the legitimation of women's suffering. But it is important to face such a challenge squarely: Has the text played its part in this unfortunate history, and if so, does that mean we should resist and reject this text and its ethical perspective, or are there ways to re-read it without allowing it such negative influence? Just as the abolitionists and anti-apartheid readers of the Bible raised critical questions that helped to shake particular and oppressive construals of biblical teaching, so new questions and criticisms continue to provoke ongoing reflection.

Conclusion: 1 Peter and the Making of Christian Identity

1 Peter, then, like all the New Testament texts to greater or lesser degree, leaves an ambivalent legacy, offering positive resources to contemporary theology and ethics, but also requiring nuanced and critical appropriation. I want to conclude by returning to a historical perspective on the letter, summarizing the reasons why I find 1 Peter to be a particularly interesting and important text for its contribution to the process of making what we now know as Christianity.

First, more than any other New Testament text, 1 Peter represents a drawing together of a wide range of Jewish and early Christian traditions: using the Jewish scriptures extensively, adopting Gospel and Pauline material, and sharing traditions with James and with other early Christian literature (see Chapter 2). This kind of consolidation and synthesis of diverse early Christian tradition was, as the influential historian of early Christianity Ferdinand Christian Baur pointed out long ago, a crucial step in the bringing together of often conflicting approaches and in the making of what would become Christian orthodoxy.

Second, 1 Peter presents a particularly rich and important example of a widespread early Christian strategy: applying the scriptural descriptions of the people of God to the new converts of the Christian movement (see Chapter 4). As we noted before, 1 Pet. 2.9-10 is a climactic point in this process, significant not least in its application of the term *genos* (race, tribe) to the Christians, a concept which later became widespread and fundamental to Christian self-understanding as members of a 'third race'.

Third, 1 Peter offers rich insight into the ways in which Christians sought to negotiate their existence and identity in a hostile world. 1 Peter's particular response to this challenge is to call for 'good' behaviour which will minimize offence and hostility, while at the same time drawing clear limits around the extent to which loyalty can be offered to Rome: the emperor may be honoured, but not worshipped (see Chapter 5). Once again, this stance of what I have called polite resistance - being loyal citizens but within clear limits - became an established stance for Christians in the empire, and specifically those facing martyrdom.

Fourth, 1 Peter provides an illuminating glimpse into the contexts in which the name 'Christian' was used, and, crucially, takes the first steps towards claiming this label as a positive one that insiders can proudly bear (see Chapter 5). Again, then, 1 Peter makes a crucial and early contribution to a process that was of central significance in the emergence of Christianity - namely the eventual adoption of 'Christian' as the standard self-designation.

For all these reasons, and more, 1 Peter deserves to be rescued from its marginal status in New Testament studies. John Elliott and others have already done a great deal to try to secure this rescue, and to rehabilitate this short letter. I hope that this guide will make its own small contribution to this task, and will enable readers to appreciate - though not uncritically - this fascinating early Christian epistle.

Further Reading

For Luther's positive comments on 1 Peter, see:

> Luther, Martin, *Commentary on Peter and Jude*, ed. John N. Lenker (Grand Rapids, MI: Kregel, 1990 [1523]).

Marshall's (1991) commentary is listed in Chapter 1, as are those of Achtemeier (1996) and Elliott (2000). For valuable treatments of the theology of 1 Peter, from which comments in this chapter are taken, see also:

> Marshall, I. Howard, *New Testament Theology* (Downers Grove, IL: InterVarsity Press, 2004).

> Martin, Ralph P., '1 Peter', in Andrew N. Chester and Ralph P. Martin, *The Theology of the Letters of James, Peter and Jude* (Cambridge: Cambridge University Press, 1994), 87-133.

Lindbeck's comments on the relationship between the Church and Israel are to be found in:

> Lindbeck, George, 'What of the Future? A Christian Response', in Tikva Frymer-Kensky et al. (eds), *Christianity in Jewish Terms* (Boulder: Westview, 2000), 357-66.

A critical view of 1 Peter's imperialist strategy in usurping Judaism's identity is presented in:

> Bauman-Martin, Betsy J., 'Postcolonial Aliens and Strangers in 1 Peter', in Robert L. Webb and Betsy Bauman-Martin

(eds), *Reading 1 Peter with New Eyes: Methodological Reassessments of the Letter of First Peter* (LNTS; London and New York: T&T Clark, 2007).

For discussions of the complex process by which Christianity and Judaism became distinct and often antagonistic religions, and of the NT's impact on the development of anti-Semitism, see, from among a large literature:

Dunn, James D.G., *The Partings of the Ways* (London: SCM, 1991).

Dunn, James D.G. (ed.), *Jews and Christians: The Parting of the Ways A.D. 70 to 135* (Tübingen: Mohr Siebeck, 1992).

Gager, John G., *The Origins of Anti-Semitism* (Oxford: Oxford University Press, 1983).

Wilson, Stephen G., *Related Strangers: Jews and Christians, 70-170 C.E.* (Minneapolis, MN: Fortress, 1995).

Corley's feminist reading of 1 Peter is found in:

Corley, Kathleen, '1 Peter', in Elisabeth Schüssler Fiorenza (ed.), *Searching the Scriptures, Vol. 2: A Feminist Commentary* (London: SCM, 1995), 349-60.

Somewhat more sympathetic treatments of 1 Peter's instructions to social conformity can be found, for example, in the essays of Carter and Volf listed in Chapter 5.

Discussions of NT ethics in the light of the use of the material to justify slavery in the American South and apartheid in South Africa, together with proposals for more morally acceptable ways to use the Bible in ethics, are presented by:

Burridge, Richard A., *Imitating Jesus: An Inclusive Approach to New Testament Ethics* (Grand Rapids, MI: Eerdmans, 2007).

Meeks, Wayne A., 'The "Haustafeln" and American Slavery: A Hermeneutical Challenge', in Eugene H. Lovering Jr and

Jerry L. Sumney (eds), *Theology and Ethics in Paul and His Interpreters: Essays in Honor of Victor Paul Furnish* (Nashville, TN: Abingdon, 1996), 232-53.

Barth's comments on the task of dogmatic theology are found in:

Barth, Karl, *Church Dogmatics*, Vol. I.1 (trans. G.W. Bromiley; Edinburgh: T&T Clark, 2nd edn, 1975).

More generally, on the uses of the Bible in Christian theology, see:

Kelsey, David H., *The Uses of Scripture in Recent Theology* (London: SCM, 1975).

Watson, Francis, *Text, Church and World: Biblical Interpretation in Theological Perspective* (Edinburgh: T&T Clark, 1994).

And on the diversity of approaches practised in contemporary biblical criticism, see:

Haynes, Stephen R. and Steven L. McKenzie (eds), *To Each Its Own Meaning: An Introduction to Biblical Criticisms and Their Application* (Louisville, KY: Westminster John Knox, 1993).

INDEXES

Index of References

Page numbers in bold type indicate a significant discussion of that text.

Other Early Jewish Literature

New Testament

Index of Authors

Page numbers in bold type indicate a discussion of that author's work.

Index of Subjects

Page numbers in bold type indicate a significant discussion of that topic.